THE BOYS' DUMAS
G. A. Henty: aspects of Victorian Publishing

by

John Cargill Thompson

TO
NYM

Author's note: In the text there are various references to my book *Hentyana*. Due to the current financial situation this book has yet to appear.

Copyright © John Cargill Thompson 1975

SBN 85635 144 X

First published 1975 by
Carcanet Press Limited
266 Councillor Lane
Cheadle Hulme, Cheadle
Cheshire SK8 5PN

Printed in Great Britain by Eyre & Spottiswoode Ltd.

CONTENTS

Henty or Hendy is a name derived from the Anglo-Saxon and means a combination of gentle and courteous. In Chaucer's *Canterbury Tales*, the host reproves the Friar:

> Sire you should be a hende,
> And curteis as a man of your estate.

PREFACE

My first book on George Henty, *Hentyana*, was intended as a probe for bibliographical and biographical information. Even in manuscript it brought me into contact with others engaged on a similar task, but Henty had eluded us all. We knew roughly where he was at certain points in his life and numerous anecdotes survived but the picture was too obscure for any of us to feel ready to tackle a biography; rather we wished to evoke his shadow and from this, perhaps, learn more of the nature of this extraordinary man.

The Bibliographical picture remains clouded. In some cases the first edition has still to be established and it is possible that there is a considerable amount still to be discovered. With a collection of over 2,000 variant Henty editions, I am in a strong position to engage in bibliographical description, yet additions to my collection tend to pose further questions rather than clarify the picture. I estimate my collection at something under 6 per cent of the total number of variations in existence, hence the speculative nature of my introduction. This is the kind of material exchanged by Henty collectors and enthusiasts.

The sections on American editions are still far from complete but I am assured by American collectors that they are the most complete surveys of their kind in existence. The collector and the bookseller have indulged in a kind of poker over these editions, both sides being equally in the dark. These sections aim to clarify this confusion.

In all cases right and left refer to book right (spine) and not the reader's right.

Finally I would like to acknowledge the assistance of the late Captain R. L. Dartt, the Rev. A. B. E. Brown, Mr William Allan, Mr Christopher Hunt, Mr Vernon Askew and Mrs Elizabeth Spring.

John Cargill Thompson, 1974.

Introduction

The fascination of collecting Henty

G. A. Henty (1832–1902) is one of the most collectable of authors, one of the main reasons being his colossal output. This combined with the variety of editions makes the achievement of a complete collection of Henty titles difficult and of variant editions, impossible. The bulk of his work is not difficult to obtain in some sort of format and even the first editions, for the most part, hardly qualify as rare books. Thus the novice collector can quite easily achieve a relatively satisfying collection, but then it begins to get exciting.

There have been three major bibliographical contributions. The first was a check list of 149 titles compiled by Stanley A. Pachon in the January 1949 *Dime Novel Roundup*. There are of course many omissions and it makes no attempt at bibliographical description but it does contain one useful aid to memory dropped from future check lists: the name of the hero in brackets, a typical entry being:

13 By England's Aid; or, The Freeing of the Netherlands (1585–1604) (Hero: Lionel Vickers) Blackie 1891, Burt, Conkey, Federal, Hurst, Mershon, S. & S. Medal No. 176 1902, Scribner, Winston.

Although this did not help collectors to identify first editions it did provide a guide to the American pirate publications. Twenty-five years later after considerable bibliographical activity the following additional publishers can be added to the known pirate editions of this title: Allison, Donohue, International, Lupton and Mutual. There is also an interesting variant title by Superior, *With England's Aid*.

The next step was taken by R. S. Kennedy and B. J. Farmer, with their *Bibliography of G. A. Henty & Hentyana*. This concentrated on first and principal editions, supplying a bibliographical description and an indication of value. This latter was a very great mistake. What it really meant was 'this is what I would pay for a copy' or 'this is what I paid for my copy'. It certainly did not mean 'if you sell your copy you will get £x'. The valuations given by

Kennedy and Farmer encouraged some people to collect Henty as an investment rather than from interest. There were many ommissions and slight errors of description but most of today's larger Henty collections are based on this work. The *By England's Aid* entry, in comparison to Pachon's checklist, reads:

BY ENGLAND'S AID: 1891.

By England's Aid:/ or / The Freeing of the Netherlands./ (1585–1604) / By / G. A. Henty,/ Author of (list of titles) / With ten page illustrations by Alfred Pearse,/and four maps./ publisher's device/ Blackie & Son, Limited,/ London, Glasgow, Edinburgh, and Dublin./ 1891.

Crown 8vo., 5 × 7¼ inches; maroon endpapers; half-title; frontispiece; title page as above; preface; contents; list of illustrations; text pp. (II) to 384; 32 pp. of Messrs Blackie's catalogue; endpapers.

Variant bindings of brown or dark blue cloth-covered boards, bevelled, with decorated front: man on horseback; and spine: full-length picture of armed man. Lettering in gold. Leaves burnished olivine edges.

Also published by Blackie in Canada and by Charles Scribner's Sons, New York.

Value of the first edition: 30/–

There are two errors in the description of the title page – or) or, (or,; and (1585–1604)) (1585–1604). – errors as small as this might seem irrelevant but it is variant minor detail of this kind which makes Henty so fascinating. Again, errors of this type cast doubt on the whole bibliography, so that any entry, like that for *in the Hands of the Malays* which gives the title page address as:

London Glasgow Dublin/Bombay

as against the first edition address in fifteen copies inspected:

London Glasgow Dublin Bombay

cannot be accepted.

The confusing 'Also published by Blackie in Canada and by Charles Scribner's Sons, New York' is due to ignorance rather than carelessness and can be overlooked.

What Kennedy and Farmer did very well was to outline the task before the collector. They not only included all the most interesting editions of which they were aware, but they gave examples of translations into other languages and listed some items which contained references to Henty (Hentyana). The picture they drew was sketchy and incomplete but there was no pretension towards scholarship, it was a compilation by two collectors for other collectors, nothing more.

Robert L. Dartt's *G. A. Henty: A Bibliography* is equally inadequate but somehow seems to inhibit rather than enlarge the collector's horizons. His entries which purport to describe both the British and the American firsts are confusing to the collector with either only American firsts or only British firsts. The fun and excitement is in the differences and any attempt to compress, which obscures these differences, is to say the least a pity. The fault here almost certainly lies with the publisher who for economic reasons wished to limit the size of the book. An adequate entry for *By England's Aid* would surely describe the three editions with claims to being 'first'. The British first published by Blackie in 1891 and the two American first editions. Some collectors believe the edition issued by Worthington dated 1890 could have been published with Henty's agreement, a belief based on two curious Worthington editions. The first is an undated edition of *By Pike and Dyke* which has the Blackie publisher's device above the Worthington address on its title page. The second is an edition of *With Clive in India* (*c.* 1890), the spine of this edition is a redrawn version of the spine of the Blackie first, the cover design is based on the Gordon Browne frontispiece for *With Wolfe in Canada* 1887, the publisher on the spine is 'Williams' but the address on the title page reads New York/Worthington Company/747 Broadway/. The use of the Blackie cover and publisher's device by Worthington could be interpreted as evidence of an official arrangement between the companies. 1890 was an important year with companies taking up new attitudes to the publishing of English titles because of the copyright Act. Worthington may have made a bid to become Henty's official U.S. publishers. The N. D. Scribner and Welford edition is generally accepted to be the U.S. first, the earliest catalogues indicating publication in the autumn of 1890. There is a slight possibility of a dated 1890 Scribner and Welford edition although a diligent search has failed to establish the existence of such an edition. There are also two significant editions prized by collectors of Henty 'firsts'. The first Canadian publication issued by Blackie in association with two Toronto publishers, William Briggs and The Copp, Clark Company, this is in a similar but slightly cheaper format to that of Blackie or Scribner's. It is undated on the title page but carries the following in the verso of the title page:

> Entered according to Act of the Parliament of Canada, in the year one thousand eight hundred and ninety-six, by Blackie & Son, Limited, at the Department of Agriculture.

The first Blackie–Scribner publication of this title is also valued. There may even have been a further significant edition in the

Blackie's Colonial Library. This was a uniform edition of several of Blackie's better known authors bound in dark green cloth with light green decoration 'for circulation only in India and the British Colonies'. It was also published in paper wrappers. The only Henty titles definitely established as having been included in this series are No. 1 *With Clive in India* 1896; No. 2 *A Final Reckoning*; No. 7 *When London Burned*; No. 8 *The Dash for Khartoum*, but as these four titles were all included in the first twelve volumes published others must almost certainly have followed. As the Colonial Library is the rarest of the principal Henty editions the title page of *With Clive in India* is given below for purposes of comparison:

> *Blackie's Colonial Library*/ With Clive in India/ or the/ Beginnings of an Empire/ By/ G. A. Henty/ Author of 'The Lion of the North', 'Through the Fray', 'In Freedom's Cause',/ 'True to the Old Flag', 'For Name and Fame', 'Facing Death', &c./publishers device/ London/ Blackie & Son, Limited, 50 Old Bailey, E.C./ Glasgow and Dublin/ 1896/ line/ This edition is for circulation only in India/ and the British Colonies/

It is of course unfair to criticize a book for its errors of omission due to compression or even for its errors due to ignorance, as Dartt himself says:

> That there will be errata is obvious. The Writer, however, believes that a start must be made somewhere. Understandably the compilation of so much detail will result in errors of omission or commission.

The problem with Dartt's bibliography is that the errors discovered so far are for the most part minor errors of description that cast doubts on the validity of the work. The entry for *By England's Aid* is comparatively correct although he omits the comma after 'Pearse' on the title page and seems unaware of by far the commonest cover colour for first editions of this title (Red), also Blackie and Son) Blackie & Son. He describes a variant with the '49 Old Bailey' address in place of that described by Kennedy and Farmer. The Kennedy and Farmer description address corresponds with the other Henty titles published by Blackie in 1891 (1890), while the '49 Old Bailey' address appears on titles published between 1892 and 1895, thus indicating that Dartt's copy is the second issue.

A typical title page description in Dartt's Bibliography is that for *By Pike and Dyke*:

> By Pike and Dyke/ A Tale of the Rise of the Dutch Republic/ By/ G. A. Henty,/ Author of (list of titles)/ With 10 full-page

illustrations by Maynard Brown/ and four maps/ publisher's device/ London:/ Blackie and Son, 49 and 50 Old Bailey, E.C./ Glasgow, Edinburgh, and Dublin./ 1890.

There are seven errors in this description which should read:

By Pike and Dyke:/ A Tale of the Rise of the Dutch Republic./ By/ G. A. Henty,/ Author of (list of titles)/ With full-page illustrations by Maynard Brown,/ and four maps./ publisher's device/ London:/ Blackie & Son, 49 & 50 Old Bailey, E.C./ Glasgow, Edinburgh, and Dublin./ 1890./

Every collector then must be his own bibliographer and while Pachon, Farmer and Kennedy and Dartt have provided useful check lists the detailed work still remains to be done.

It is not sufficient to have one example of the first edition of any title: one must have all the variants. Obvious differences to look for are of cover colour and endpapers, the catalogues at the back can vary between issues (one can also have undated reissues of the title with the first edition catalogue, indicating a title's extreme popularity) but there are other subtleties. We have already noted the change of address in *By England's Aid* but perhaps as fascinating as any is the case of *Under Wellington's Command*.

There are at least five variant first editions of this title:

(a) The American first, published by Charles Scribner's Sons, New York. 1898. Almost certainly printed in America with different pagination from the other firsts it bears no relation to the other variants.
(b) Published by Blackie & Son, London 1899. 32 page catalogue for Christmas 1898. Page 383 (the last page of text) has no indication of where the book was printed.
(c) As above. Page 383 after 'The End' a line, then 'printed by Blackie and Son, Limited'.
(d) As b. Except 32 page catalogue for Christmas 1899.
(e) Published by Blackie & Son, London and William Briggs/ The Copp Clarke Co., Limited, 1899. Blackie's 32 page catalogue for Christmas 1898. Page 383 after 'The End' a line, then 'printed by Blackie and Son, Limited'.

The relationship between (c) and (e) is obvious and it is interesting to note that (c) was acquired in Canada.

As satisfying as the search for variants of known firsts is the discovery of titles unrecorded by the bibliographers. Henty short stories known and unknown are still coming to light. 'A Christmas Feast' is advertised in the *Heatherstone Magazine* (June 1907, page 13) as being among thirty-seven novels and stories included in two quarto volumes issued by the Home Publishing Company, 52 Duane Street, New York. This story is almost certainly the same as 'A Noteable Christmas Dinner' reported in the December 1901 number of *Sunny South*, an American publication better known to collectors of Horatio Alger. Page 7 of the first number of *Lamberts Monthly* advertises G. A. Henty as a future contributor and 'A Sharks' Fin: or a Tale of a Life Buoy.' appears on pp. 55–58 of the third half yearly volume.

Other recorded appearances of 'A Shark's Fin' are in *A Dozen All Told*, published by Blackie in 1894 and *Twenty Novelettes* by twenty prominent novelists published by George Munro, New York, 1890 and Frank P. Lovell and Company, New York, 1899. Both Farmer and Dartt give an almost identical and unsatisfactory entry under this heading. Dartt states that no copies were available for examination. It is just possible that the 1890 date is wrong and that there is a connection between *Lambert's Monthly* and the American *Twenty Novelettes*.

The abridged Henty titles produced by Blackie as readers are well known but his work also appears in other readers:

Blackie's Model Readers Book IV. (*c.* 1895–1900)
Title Page: Blackie's/ Model Readers/ Book .IV./
Apple decoration/ London/ Blackie & Son .Ltd 50 ' Old Bailey/ .Glasgow & Dublin./
   (The type contained within a decorative frame of an apple tree.)
Cover: Green cloth covered boards. Leaf decoration (light green) Title (light green). ¼ (light green). Publisher (dark green on light green incorporated into the decoration)
Spine: Title (lettered vertically in light green).
Edges and boards: plain.
Endpapers: cream.
Contents: 17.5 cm. × 11.5 cm. Coloured frontispiece/ title page as above, decoration of two children in medieval dress eating apples on verso/ contents, continued on verso/ text pp. 7–208/ Exercises in Composition and Grammar pp. 213–239/ Notes: p. 240/
Catalogue: nil.

Henty's story 'The Christians to the Lions' (from *Beric the Briton*) is on pp. 156–165.
and

The Century Readers. Reader V (*c.* 1890)
Title Page: The/ Century Readers./ Reader V. (*This line enclosed in black frame*)/ publisher's device/ Blackie & Son, 49 & 50 Old Bailey, E.C./ Glasgow, Edinburgh and Dublin./

Cover: Red cloth-covered boards. Leaf and berry design. Black lettering (The Century Readers./ No. V – 1s – 6d./ Blackie & Son, Publishers./)
Spine: Design as on cover. Black lettering (Fifth – Reader.).
Edges and boards: plain.
Endpapers: Grey – green. 4 pp. (numbered) catalogue of Blackie & Son's Educational works. P. 4 advertises *The Sovereign Reader*, which helps to set the date of this book as after 1887.
Contents: 17.3 cm. × 11.5 cm. Frontispiece/ title page as above, preface on verso/ contents/ text: pp. (I) – 256.
No separate publisher's catalogue.

Henty's contribution 'The Golden Hind – A Story of the Time of Drake' (adapted from *Under Drake's Flag*) is on pp. 139–208.

It is very unlikely that these are the only examples of Henty in Blackie school books. Nor is it essential that work by Henty will be signed. Henty's association with Blackie did not start until 1882, but he very quickly established himself as Blackie's main writer for boys. He was given a colossal build up in their publisher's catalogues with his books being given priority to those of any other author. We examine below the possibility of Henty's authorship of certain unsigned stories and articles. While most of these must still remain as puzzles we can establish the fact that Henty did not always sign his work. Blackie's constant use of his name in their advertising makes anonymous productions from this house an outside possibility, at least after 1890, but some in the 1880s ring certain bells.

We have probably discovered about one-tenth of Henty's unsigned work and the collector is strongly advised to acquire all anonymous Blackie publications that he feels could possibly contain Henty. Unusual off-centre contributions of this kind are very hard to achieve and it is better to retain books which can later be discarded than release a doubtful title which may find a place in the bibliography as new facts come to light.

The Victorians were very fond of collections of stories retold from history. These are often anonymous and show every sign of having been hastily put together perhaps by several authors. A Blackie example of this type of book is *Stirring Events of History* 1886, illustrated by John Schönberg. The 'Preface' states:

The Events of History which have been selected for the present work are many in number and varied in character. In the compilation of the volume the object has been to give a series of sketches stretching over a long term of time, rather than a finished picture of any definite period. Hence between the twelfth and nineteenth centuries will be found narratives of incidents which have occurred in various parts of the world, and under various circumstances. They have been collected during a long course of reading, and the only attempt at classification made, has been to place the articles in chronological order. The authenticity of the information given can be vouched for. Many curious and out-of-the-way books have been consulted; and in all cases where authorities have differed, an attempt has been made to reconcile them as far as possible.

The Editor has endeavoured to give a readable and interesting series of incidents in history, which may serve to engender in the minds of those who read it a desire to pursue other books of history, which, says an old English author, 'is ever most profitable reading'.

This matches Henty's own feelings about accuracy in boys' reading, as expressed in the *Union Jack* volume I, p. 384:

While the main object of all the tales will be to entertain, lads may rely upon the information conveyed in them to be trustworthy and genuine. For example, in 'In Times of Peril', every item of history, the regiments engaged, the dates of the events, and the description of the battles and sieges are absolutely authentic; similar accuracy of detail will characterize all stories that appear in the magazine.

The contents of *Stirring Events of History* would appear to be by several hands and none of the episodes are really consistent with Henty's style, but by 1886 Henty had become Blackie's main writer for boys and he could well have been asked to edit this work and write the introduction. The claim is very flimsy and circumstantial but it needs only the proof that Henty was involved in one compilation of this nature to bring a whole new range of books under consideration and collectors are well advised to put aside a shelf for 'possibles'.

It is, of course, essential to retain the ability to reject. My saddest experience along these lines was a series of articles by 'Odd Boy' in *Beeton's Boy's Book of History and Adventure* (1869). My attention was caught by an article 'A letter from an Abyssinian Prisoner' pp. 488–490. This article purported to be written by Ex-King Theodore's horse. Two unsigned articles about the Abyssinian Campaign, both written in 1868 are now established as Henty's work. Indiana possess a copy of a letter corroborating the *Cornhill* dispatch 'Camp Life in Abyssinia' (March 10, 1868). The letter was sent by Henty to the publishers, Messrs. Smith, Elder and Company, offering this contribution and enquiring if they required others. The second article is in *All the Year Round* vol. 20 pp. 254–260. This is incorrectly entered on page 21 of Dartt's

Companion as 'Mule Number (?)'. This article was established as being by Henty by Professor C. F. Willey. Willey followed up the slightest of clues that Henty had written an article for either *Household Words* or *All the Year Round* until he eventually discovered the article 'Sixty-Eight in Abyssinia', the phraseology was similar to passages in *The March to Magdala* and 'Camp Life in Abyssinia' and he finally established his case unearthing correspondence between Henty and Dickens' assistant. 'Sixty-Eight in Abyssinia' describes some of the conditions during the campaign through the eyes of a mule.

This was the link, a ghost writer for a mule might well have performed the same service for a horse! The style was nothing like Henty's usual writing for boys but if it was written in 1868 or 1869 before he had started his long series of boys' books his style could not have developed. There did seem to be traces of his rather heavy handed attempts at humour as revealed in *Those Other Animals*. Also the article is highly critical of the English in a way that was not inconsistent with my findings from his boys' books. The article was signed 'Odd Boy' the kind of pseudonym one might expect Henty to adopt. An interesting case was emerging. After all *Out on the Pampas* is an ambitious start in the new field of juvenile literature, was it not possible that he had written articles or short stories for boys prior to this?

What was Henty's connection with Ward Lock and *Beeton's Boy's Own Books*? While he was one of the most successful of writers for boys, there were others available and his record as an editor was hardly brilliant. When he took over the new *Beeton's Boy's Own Magazine* in 1889 he was at one of the busiest points of his career. It might be argued that he would be unlikely to undertake an entirely new venture, particularly one where his contribution was to be so restrained unless there was some incentive other than money.

The two Abyssinian articles referred to above, in the *Cornhill* and *All the Year Round* seem to indicate that Henty was trying in 1868 to establish an outlet for articles which seem to have been unsigned. This was the turning point in his career and my outline of this period of his life in a biography would be along the following lines:

> Returned from Abyssinia, he realizes he is now almost 37 . . . his first novel *A Search for a Secret* has made no real impact . . . he has a cupboard full of other novels and some juvenile verse, including a long poem to his wife and an embarrassing book of poems printed when he was a schoolboy . . . he is tired, more so than after previous campaigns and he now desires to be taken seriously as a writer rather than dismissed as a journalist . . .

Two leading literary journals *Cornhill* (still associated with Thackeray, although he had died five years previously) and *All the Year Round* (Dickens) accept articles by him . . . he decides to emulate Russell and publish his correspondence from Abyssinia, while also attempting a second novel *All But Lost* . . . He was able to spend more time with his family telling the children stories after dinner . . . On the advice of a friend, he works one of these stories into a book for boys which he calls *Out on the Pampas* . . . he produces numerous articles and stories many of which are consigned to the waste paper basket . . . Certainly this was a time of experiment and productivity spurred on by a sense that forty is approaching and he has not yet realized any of his earlier ambitions.

Perhaps it was at this time that he became involved with Tillotson's literary syndicate, and as John Tillotson was a regular contributor to *Beeton's Boy's Own Magazine*. This could be yet another link in the Henty–Beeton–Ward Lock puzzle.

This is the kind of speculation in which the collector revels but he must not allow his enthusiasm to blind his judgement. I desperately wanted to establish 'A letter from an Abyssinian Prisoner' as Henty's work, but there were six other articles signed 'Odd Boy' to be considered along with it.

Pp. 217–220. 'The Odd Boy on a Self-made man'. The article is precocious and would-be humorous. There are many words and phrases that are uncharacteristic of Henty e.g. 'Whither he was early sent' . . . 'Happy, thrice happy those who'. The only aspect which fitted Henty was that the article was aimed at a type of man despised by him.

Pp. 378–381. 'A Memorial to Murphies'. An unfunny article about Ireland and potatoes. Although Henty did have links with Ireland there is nothing to connect this article with his work.

Pp. 437–440. 'The Odd Boy on Everything'. This contains feeble attempts at humour in a rather adult vein. The main theme of the article is that people are becoming too soft.

Pp. 550–553. 'Hops by the Odd Boy'. A humorous article sprinkled with verse in praise of beer. Oddly enough the verse seems to me to have the same sub-Gilbertian quality of the verse letter quoted in *Hentyana*:

> Beer, beer, generous beer,
> Quaff at the tankards, there's plenty more here;
> The sweet and the bitter so nicely combine
> That who would exchange it for juice of the wine?
> . . . .
> Beer, beer, generous beer,
> Don't spare the tankard we've plenty more here;

> But, as all things must end, our song here must stop,
> With *bravo!* bravissimo!! H.O.P. Hop!!

Henty was never against young people drinking in moderation but the general feel of the article is unlike his work.

Pp. 601–604. 'The Odd Boy on Muzzled Dogs'. This article also contains a liberal sprinkling of verse. The style has changed since the first article although it is still heavy handed and would-be humorous. There is a sense of experiment as if the contributor is still trying to discover a style suitable for boys.

Pp. 649–652. 'Christmas Fare and Christmas Fairies'. An article about puddings and pantomimes unparalleled by anything in Henty's known work.

This was an unsuccessful exercise in speculation but the Henty–Beeton–Ward Lock puzzle still remains a possible source of new information. On the face of it Ward Lock would seem to be the last of Henty's juvenile publishers, apart from Blackie, and his association with them the briefest (1889–1891). Ward Lock had been very lucky and perhaps a little devious in acquiring the rights to all the work published by S. O. Beeton, as this included *Mrs Beeton's Household Management*. It also included a wealth of juvenile material and the rights of *Beeton's Boy's Own Magazine*.

It was decided to bring out a magazine under the old name, reissuing the old material with certain editing and selecting by George A. Henty. The result, six bound volumes containing the parts of a magazine which ran for only two years (1889–1890). These parts were then reissued as six bound volumes of *Beeton's Boy's Own Books*. It is at this point that the bibliographical picture becomes clouded, three other volumes of *BBOB* were published:

(7) *Stories of Adventure and Heroism*

(8) *Fact, Fiction, History and Adventure*

(9) *Brave Tales of Daring Deeds and Adventure at Home and Abroad.*

There are at least seven variants of number (7). (1) edited by G. A. H. contains: *Silas Horner's Adventures/Wild Sports of the World/Jewel Mysteries* I have known. (2) edited by G. A. H. contains: *Robinson Crusoe/Silas Horner/Brave British Soldiers and the Victoria Cross.* (3) edited by G. A. H. contains: *Silas Horner/Wild Sports of the World/Robinson Crusoe.* (4) edited by G. A. H. contains: *Silas Horner/Wild Sports of the World/Lady Turpin.*

(5), (6), (7). No credited editor, contain: *Robinson Crusoe/Silas Horner/Brave British Soldiers and The Victoria Cross.* The variations between these three examples are in frontispiece and colour of binding.

The important point here is that we have a Henty connection. A further complication is added by the fact that this title, unlike *BBOB* I–VI, is not based on the Henty edited *Beeton's Boys' Own Magazine* but on another Ward, Lock publication, *Forest, Field and Flood* which contains: *Wild Sports of the World/Brave British Soldiers and the Victoria Cross/Robinson Crusoe.* The pagination of these stories as they appear in *Forest, Field and Flood* is identical with their usage in *Adventure and Heroism,* the type face is the same and the only significant difference between the books is that all variants of *Adventure and Heroism* are in the uniform *BBOB* with its decoration of a mountain with a man riding a horse on the cover, *Forest, Field and Flood* is red cloth bevelled boards with gold lettering and decoration of a ship on the spine and a gaucho lassooing a bull, again in gold, on the cover. *Forest, Field and Flood* also contains a coloured frontispiece and coloured plates for *Robinson Crusoe,* the edges are in gold. What is Henty's connection with this work? It would seem to predate *Adventure and Heroism*, but not by much, the publisher's address on the title page is:

> London:
> Ward, Lock & Bowden Limited,
> Warwick House, Salisbury Square, E.C.
> New York and Melbourne.

which according to Dartt's *Companion* would indicate a date after 1893! A further complication, because if it is indeed later than *Adventure and Heroism* it is simply a more expensive version of a book already connected with G. A. H.

It should also be noted that variants (5), (6), and (7) of *Stories of Adventure and Heroism*, although identical in format to other *Beeton's Boys' Own Books,* do not credit Henty as editor. These would appear to be variant issues of the first publication of this title. The dated 1892 *Fact, Fiction, History and Adventure* and a similar *Brave Tales of Daring Deeds Etc.,* also carry no acknowledgment of Henty's editorship although identical in contents to later issues of these titles which carry his name as editor. Here we have what would appear to be three unacknowledged Henty firsts. Thus establishing a precedent for unsigned Henty items in the 1890's.

It would seem from the lack of material actually by Henty, in the Ward Lock publications, that his editorial involvement was slight, but this is out of character. Henty was not a man who would simply allow his name to be used to endorse a product, nor is there any evidence that he needed money at this point. The bulk of the material in *Beeton's Boys' Own Magazine* is taken from four pub-

lications issued by Ward Lock twelve years earlier; these are themselves re-issues of material from the original *Beeton's Boys' Own
Magazine* which had flourished in the 1860's and are presented as
'edited by S. O. Beeton'.

(1) *Beeton's Fact, Fiction, History and Adventure.* Containing;
*Cressy and Poictiers/A Coasting Voyage from the Thames to the
Tyne/Papers on Natural History./The Adventures of Reuben
Davidger.* a tale/Scientific articles/Chemistry/How to make a
small organ, Galvanic Battery, Model Steamer, Marine Engine,
etc./The Story of the British Navy/Up in the Alps/*The Young
Norseman*/Poetry, Puzzles, etc., etc. 1100 pages, 33 page
engravings and woodcuts in the text.
(2) *Beeton's Historical Romances, Daring Deeds, and Animal
Stories.* Containing: *Runnymede and Lincoln Fair/Antony
Waymouth/The Zoological Gardens/King Lion*/Historical
Stories/Scientific Stories/*Victoria Cross Gallery*/Sports and Pas-
times/Poetry/Puzzles/etc., etc.
(3) *Beeton's Brave Tales Bold Ballads, and Travels by Sea
and Land.* Containing: Historical stories/*Hubert Ellis/Ingony-
ma/Highland Regiments as they once were/King of
Tramps*/Poems by Beranger etc. /*Return of the Emperor*/Scien-
tific Papers Miscellaneous Papers/*Silas the Conjurer/Victoria
Cross Gallery/Sports and Pastimes/Wigs Exploits/The Zoological
Gardens.*
(4) *Beeton's Tales of Chivalry, School Stories, Mechanics at
Home and Exploits of the Army and Navy.* Containing:
Domestic Dogs/Miscellaneous articles/*Old Arms/Phil Craw-
ford*/Poetry/*Prince Jack of Figi*/Puzzle Pages/*Ralph de Wal-
den*/Rowing/Scientific Articles/*Story of the Battle of Camp St
Vincent/A Trip to Tauranga/Under the Water/Victoria Cross Gal-
lery/Weapons and Implements of Many Lands/In the Western
World/The Zoological Gardens.*

The similarity of titles and contents are immediately apparent
but a comparison between the two series is quite informative about
Henty's editing technique. His unusual system of pagination, using
letters as well as numbers, enabled the binders to divide up the
magazine parts so that a whole story could be bound consecutively
and the reader would not have to jump about a book in order to
finish a story. The paper and print are a considerable improve-
ment. The binding is brighter and more attractive. Finally it should
be noted that some new material such as *Black Man's Ghost* by J.
C. Hutcheson, a personal friend of Henty, is included. Throughout
the brief run of this magazine Henty seems to have employed his
talents in organising and administrating the paper which agrees
with the theory that he saw himself as an arbiter of boys' taste. The
Beeton's material is among the most difficult to obtain, none of the

collections, either in public or private hands, contain a complete set of all the variations together with the Ward Lock material which may or may not be significant. A full examination of the Ward Lock–Beeton–Henty triangle could throw a fascinating light in editorial and publishing techniques. A further complication is added by the publication in single volumes as *Beeton's Boys' Own Books* of several stories used in the series, e.g. 'Cressy and Poictiers'; these post date the Henty series and may or may not owe something to his editorship. A ghost title is advertised in several editions of this series: *Stories of Heroism and Adventure* and it is possible that a variant of *Stories of Adventure and Heroism* exists under this title. Bibliographically there are still many problems to be solved and other anonymous publications by Ward Lock between 1889–1893 may well be linked in some way to Henty's brief editorship of *Beeton's Boys' Own Books*.

The real collector revels in the no man's land discussed above. The fascination derives from the lack of facts. Were the biography and bibliography established and complete there would be nothing new to discover and the task would become the relatively simple matter of buying all his work. With Henty, every collector has a chance of discovering new items for himself.

Even Henty's adult writing has not come down to us in its entirety. Several copies of *Gabriel Allen M.P.* are recorded but it is significant that while the work is advertised as:

Crown 8 vo, paper cover, 1s.; cloth, 1s. 6d. each.

no copy has yet come to light in the original publisher's wrappers and those bound in cloth seem to be either rebound or in a publisher's remainder binding. Only one known copy of *Seaside Maidens* survives with the title page and in its original wrappers. Other books may well have perished completely. Farmer first mentioned *A Highland Fore* as being by Henty yet no copy has come to light. A friend of mine claims to have seen it advertised in another book but has since been unable to trace the advertisement. Captain Dartt stated in a letter to me:

I still cannot reconcile *Highland Fore* with Henty, although somewhere I saw (I believe at Cornell University) a printed leaflet which listed a half dozen or so Hentys being issued and among them was that title. Previously I had seen it on a very early catalogue by some collector (back 25 years) I think.

It's not much to go on. After all it is possible that the title is a misprint for a *Hidden Foe* or it could be *A Highland Fort* or *A Highland Foray*, but taken along with the fact that *Gabriel Allen M.P.* and *Seaside Maidens* only partially survive it should be pursued rather than ignored as a mis-statement.

A further possible novel title, although it seems most unlikely that it was ever published, is *Frank Tressilor*. This story was submitted to Chapman and Hall during the 1860's when George Meredith was one of their readers. This is referred to in B. W. Matz's article in *The Fortnightly Review* (August 2, 1909), "George Meredith as Publisher's Reader":

> . . ., although the author was again encouraged to go on, as was G. A. Henty, whose story *Frank Tressilor* was returned with instructions to 'encourage the author to send any future work.'

The hero of Henty's second published novel, *All But Lost*, Frank Maynard shares the same Christian name and it is possible this was a first draft of that story. Certainly Henty re-used a lot of his adult material in his boys' books, *Captain Bayley's Heir* is a rewrite of *All But Lost* and *One of the 28th* is based on *A Search for A Secret*, so that almost certainly any 'lost' adult work survives somewhere among his canon. A letter presumably to Meredith mentions this work and a two-volume book on the Liberation of Italy. I am unable to trace the owner of this valuable document, the copy in my possession having no provenance.

Three unsigned stories presumably by Henty, each with separate pagination are bound into Henty's personal copy of *Seaside Maidens* now in the Indiana University collection. These are 'A Simple Story', pp. (472)–480; 'Coming Together', pp. (182)–192; and 'The King of Clubs', pp. (235)–240. The source of these stories has yet to be traced but they also indicate the existence of other unsigned items. Obviously it is most likely that these would occur in books published by firms known to have connections with Henty. The most significant item of this kind is the Sampson Low, Marston one volume edition of *Bevis*. Any other anonymously edited work from this publishing house and roughly contemporary deserves consideration. As for example *Stories of Strange Adventures* by Captain Mayne Reid and others. Further evidence might possibly establish one or more of these stories as the work of Henty and it is not inconsistent with the evidence still being discovered that he could have selected the collection. Again we have a volume to add to our shelf of possibles which we may later find ourselves rejecting.

Henty's career as an editor of boys' journals is worthy of much closer study.

A few months after Kingston started *The Union Jack* at the end of part 18, April 29, 1880, he wrote:

> With much regret I have to bid you farewell. The task I undertook has been far more laborious than I expected and prevents

me from accomplishing my other important duties. I have therefore transferred it to younger and abler hands, though I hope
still to contribute to the paper . . . I have now to bespeak your
favour for a successor. Mr Henty is well known to boys as the
author of those capital books *The Young Buglers, The Young
Franc-Tireurs* and *Out on the Pampas*. He is still more widely
known as the Special Correspondent of the Standard Newspaper. He was with the British Army in the Crimea, accompanied the Abyssinians and Ashanti expedition and has wit-
nessed all the European wars which have taken place during the
last twenty years.

allowing that Henty was contributing two serials *Times of Peril*
(later *In Times of Peril*) and *Facing Death* to the first volume of
Union Jack, he was still virtually unknown to the juvenile reading
public. There is something paternalistic in the way Kingston
handed over the succession to Henty who assumed the mantle
almost as though it were a sacred trust. In the next part he introduced himself 'To the Readers of the *Union Jack*',

Dear Lads – I fancy that most of us in our secret hearts cherish a
longing for something or other, but . . . it is not often that these
wishes are gratified . . . I am an example of a boy who has got his
wish; for I have very often thought that I should . . . like to edit a
magazine for boys.
   The editor of a boys' magazine should have a great liking for,
and a keen sympathy with boys. He should have the art of
putting himself in their place, and of feeling what they feel, and
liking what they like. In this way only can he choose stories that
will take. For a story may be excellent in itself, admirable in
tone, well written, and with plenty of plot, and yet it may fail
altogether with boys, simply because, as they would say themselves, it does not suit them.

Henty also re-issued Kingston's *Our Sailors* and *Our Soldiers*.
My own 1882 copy of *Our Sailors* is identical in contents to those
bearing Henty's name on the title page but gives no indication of
his participation. The title page of my copy reading:

Our Sailors/Anecdotes of the Engagements and Gallant Deeds
of the British Navy/During the Reign of/Her Majesty Queen
Victoria/By/William H. G. Kingston/Author of 'Our Soldiers',
'Peter the Whaler', 'Mark Seaworth'/'True Blue', etc./pub-
lisher's device/Griffith and Farran/successors to Newbury and
Harris/Corner of St Paul's Churchyard, London/E. P. Dutton
and Co.,/New York/.

This book contains two catalogues, the first part of the original
gathering of the book and advertising *Out on the Pampas* as having

just been published in the Boys' Own Favourite Library, the second bound in and dated 1882. Here then is another boys' book edited by Henty but without any indication of his involvement. The Uniform Boys' Own Favourite Library *Our Soldiers* (also 1882) carries the line 'edited and brought down to date by G. A. Henty' on the title page. This carries a slightly earlier catalogue than that bound into *Our Sailors*. Page 5 advertises The Boys' Own Favourite Library and contains the entry:

Our Sailors. By W. H. G. Kingston. Revised and brought down to date by G. A. Henty.

Here would seem to be a repeat of the practice, shown in Section II to have been employed by Sampson Low, in connection with *Bevis*, of advertising an editor's connection with a book but not necessarily indicating this on the title page.

An interesting anonymous series published by Griffith and Farran was 'Taking Tales' edited by the late W. H. G. Kingston. We have noted that Henty had taken over some of Kingston's commitments with this publishing house and it is not impossible that he should have undertaken responsibility for this series:

Suitable for School and Parish Libraries, etc.
TAKING TALES
Edited by the late W. H. G. Kingston.
Each Tale complete in one volume of 64 pp. crown 8vo size, cloth elegant, in large clear type, fully illustrated, 6d. each.
The object of this Series is to supply the cottagers and humbler classes of England, whose knowledge of reading and vocabularies are limited with books in clear, large type, composed of words the meaning of which they understand, sentences which the eye can take in with ease, ideas suited to their comprehension, on subjects likely to excite their interest, so that they may obtain amusement and wholesome instruction without the labour which a large number of the works at present put into their hands demands.
The Series (Tales) will be found suitable for the poorer population of our towns, the inhabitants of our coasts, and our soldiers and sailors in barracks and on board ship; also for reading in night schools.
The following are the titles of the volumes in the series:
The Miller of Hillbrook; Tom Trueman, the Sailor; The Fortunes of Michael Hale and his Family; John Armstrong, the Soldier; Joseph Rudge, the Australian Shepherd; Life Underground, or Dick the Colliery Boy; Life on the Coast, or The Little Fisher Girl; Adventures of Two Orphans in London; Early Days on Board a Man-of-War; Walter the Foundling; The Tenants of Sunneyside Farm; Holmwood, or The New Zealand Settler.

An examination of one of these, *Walter the Foundling* revealed striking similarities of style to the known work of Henty. The historical detail and information contained in the story made little concession to the announcement, quoted above, nor was the hero such as would appeal to 'the cottagers and humbler classes'.

The foundling becomes the squire of a Saxon Knight, Sir Nigel. On the way to a tournament they rescue the Lady Ethel from an attack by some robbers. Walter and later the Lady Ethel are kidnapped by a Norman baron who wishes to marry the Lady Ethel. Walter makes his escape and rescues the Lady. It comes to light that he is her brother and the real heir to her estates. The last paragraph is typical of the final paragraphs of Henty's historical novels:

> Both Sir Nigel and Sir Walter were among the barons who at the famous meeting on the 15th of June, 1215, on Runnymede, near Windsor compelled the most graceless of sovereigns, King John, to sign the Magna Carta, which may well be called the groundwork of English liberty. Few more rejoiced to see that day than the Saxon Tostig. He and his descendants gained many advantages by it, and though slavery was not yet abolished, its fate was sealed, happily to be brought about in the generation following.

The central theme of a foundling who is really of noble birth is of course common to many Victorian writers (J. C. Edgar had used it to great effect in *Cressy and Poictiers*) but it is handled in a manner not inconsistent with Henty's style.

An informative paragraph typical of the story and also of Henty appears on page 24:

> He told him that these wars were so called because the cross was the emblem or sign of the Christians, which in French, the language spoken by the chief leaders, is called *croix*, hence croixade changed into crusade.

There is friction between Saxon and Norman but the anti-semitism which is to be found in some Victorian authors but not present in Henty, is also absent from this work. Page 30:

> We differ in our faith, but I do not consider that such gives me any right to tyrannize over or ill treat you.

It should be noted that an earlier example of this tolerant attitude is *Ivanhoe* and Scott is, of course, a main model for Victorian writers. Finally it should be noted that Walter's escape through the roof of his prison, described on pages 50–51 is similar to numerous treatments of the same situation in Henty's tales.

Other clues to yet undiscovered work by Henty abound. Melton

Prior mentions an article written by him during the Ashanti campaign on the subject of a lizard sucking the blood out of a rat
(*Campaigns of a War Correspondent 1912*). It is known that he
was involved, as editor, in the *United Service Gazette*, in 1884–85.
The main evidence for Henty's editorial connection with this publication is the series of eight letters, known as G. A. Henty letters
1–8: Wolseley Autograph Collection, quoted with the permission
of the Borough Librarian and Curator, Hove Public Library.

Received by Lord Wolseley 23/6/74
                                                23 St Ann's Villas
                                                Notting Hill
                                                June 22.

Dear Sir Garnet,
    I do not suppose that you in any way concern yourself with
what the papers may say concerning the Ashanti business, but I
am writing to you for my own sake as I should be sorry that you
should think, as you reasonably might think that the article
which appeared in the Standard on Saturday was written by me.
I never write leading articles in the paper, and have today been
to the Editor to protest against the article in question as being
absolutely opposed to my letters and my book, in both of which
I stated as my opinion that a longer stay of the troops at
Coomassie would have been not only useless but dangerous in
the extreme. I objected to the whole tone of their remarks about
Glover because although I believe him to be a most energetic
and able officer, I consider, as I told Goldsworthy last week, that
his expedition was a gigantic blunder, and that it in no way
affected the issue of the campaign. The duty of a Special Correspondent is at all times difficult, and military men naturally consider the criticisms of civilians to be impertinent as they are
often eroneous. At the same time I am quite willing to bear the
cross and unpopularity of what I write, knowing that I write at
least conscientiously and to the best of my ability, but I object
very strongly to bear the cross of what I do not write. I fear that
you will consider this note to be altogether unnecessary and
uncalled for, but I received so much kindness from you out in
the Coast, that I do not like to think that you should imagine
that upon my return I should be capable of writing such articles
on the expedition as that which appeared in the Standard on
Saturday. It is no doubt a matter of indifference to you but it is
of importance to me.
    Apologies for troubling you in the matter
        I remain, dear Sir Garnet
            Yours faithfully
            G. A. Henty

This next letter was probably written in 1876 after Henty had
returned from the Turco-Servian War. It is known that his health

broke down after this campaign and except for his visit to California he did no further work outside the United Kingdom.

> 23 St Ann's Villas
> Notting Hill
> Oct. 20th

Dear Sir Garnet

I regret that I am unable to accept your kind invitation for Monday evening but I am not yet able to sit up for any time. I have been nearly three weeks in bed, and am now picking up strength fast, but I have not as yet been out of the house. I hope by the end of next week to be about again. Turkey is at present an interesting spot and is likely I think to become still more so. I do not know that I can give you any more information beyond that in my letter but should you like to ask me any questions about it, I will call at the W.O. (War Office) any day and time, after next week, which may suit you.

> Yours very truly
> G. A. Henty

The next letter has been endorsed by Lord Wolseley that he replied to it on 9.2.84.

9/2/84

> 103 Upper Richmond Road,
> Putney,
> Saturday.

Dear Lord Wolseley

I am sure that you will not be offended by my saying that your kind invitation places me in a dilemma. As you are aware I do a great deal of military writing for the Standard, and rightly or wrongly my opinions as to the efficiency of our army, and the effect of the changes which have been introduced differ very widely from your own. I feel then that I should be placed in a false position by accepting your hospitality, when I may the next day be called upon to express opinions diametrically opposed to your views and to criticize unfavourably changes and modifications which have your approval. I am sure that you agree with me that under the circumstances it is best that I should frankly say that while appreciating warmly the kindness of your invitation, I feel myself unable to avail myself of it for the reasons I have given.

> I remain, Dear Lord Wolseley
> Yours truly
> G. A. Henty

General Lord Wolseley K.G.B.

The next in the collection is simply dated August 15th. All the evidence indicates that it was written in 1885. Wolseley returned to London from Khartoum on 13.7.85. Hove Public Library have an envelope which seems likely to belong to this letter which is post-marked 16.8.85. This is the letter which establishes Henty's connection with *The United Services Gazette*.

> The United Services Gazette
> 6 Catherine Street
> W.C.
> August 15th

Dear Lord Wolseley,
   Permit me to add my congratulations to the many which you must have received upon your safe return home, and the honours which you have won. I am now Editor of the above paper, and in to-days issue have ventured to express my appreciation of your work. I wrote to Sir A. Alison when I assumed the reins here, and said that so long as I remained here, there would be no renewal of the very hostile tone to the War Office which had previously marked the paper. I need not repeat that to you, but my view of the matter is that a Service paper has scarcely the same freedom of criticism that other newspaper possess, as it is contrary to all disciplines for a journal read by men of all ranks in the service persistently to attack the doings and decisions of the heads of that service. Criticism is one thing, persistent hostility another. I am glad to say that since I have taken the paper I have been able to do a little to show how unfounded were the attacks upon our friend Sir John McNeill.
   I remain, dear Lord Wolseley
> Yours very truly
> G. A. Henty

General Lord Wolseley.

The next letter endorsed by Wolseley has having been replied to 22.8.85. This is one of the most fascinating surviving pieces of Henty manuscript. It establishes him as a man who expected to have his ideas listened to at the highest level.

> 103 Upper Richmond Road
> Putney.
> August 20th

Dear Lord Wolseley,
   Thanks for your most interesting letter on a matter which is undoubtedly of supreme importance to the army. That selection is theoretically an infinitely better method of obtaining good commanding officers than is seniority is I should think beyond argument. The whole question turns upon the manner of selection. In other professions promotion is the result of what may be called general approval. The Doctor rises to the head of his profession because the public recognizes his skill and flock to his consulting rooms, the Barrister obtains a great practice and

finally a judgeship because solicitors recognizing his merits, load him with briefs and push him on to distinction. The Bishop chooses a clergyman for a living (that is where there is no favouritism in the case) from the good reports he hears of his zeal and ability and by the evidence of his crowded church and successful appeals for aid for parish work. But how is the selection to be made for regimental commands? Of ten officers in ten regiments nothing whatever can be known by the appointing authorities save by the reports by the commanding officer, a report tinged in many cases by personal likes and dislikes. The Inspecting General can in his hasty visits certainly form no sufficient judgement on the merits of the individual officer. Except indeed in service in the field, and even then the chances of distinction come but seldom to Regimental officers, there is no way by which an officer can show himself superior to his fellows save by employment on the staff. In times of peace a staff officer is always under the eyes of the head of his department or the general of his district, in war his chances of mention in despatches on general orders are as twenty to one in comparison with those of a regimental officer of the same rank. Hence the staff would come to be considered the sole channel of promotion, and bad as seniority may be, I should say that promotion from the staff hampered by favouritism would be even more disastrous for the army. This would appear to me to be the difficulty, and it is in fact found to be so in the French army. I had this week in the U.S. Gazette a translation of an article from a French military paper showing that promotion by selection was in fact a lottery depending chiefly upon the amount of interest and importance of the Generals commanding the various districts. So far I have never seen any scheme for promotion by selection which grappled in earnest with this difficulty. For myself, democratic and unwieldy as such a solution may seem, especially as coming from a Tory. I believe that the very best method of selecting majors from the captains, and Lieutenant-Colonels from the majors would be by the vote of the non-commissioned officers and the privates of over three years service. These men appraise with wonderful accuracy the qualities and character of their officers. They know which are the best drill, which the most careful at inspection, which the most even tempered, the most understanding and impartial in investigating complaints, the men who are strict and yet just. I know that it would be contrary to military discipline that a choice should be made in such a way, but I am very sure that if a general order were issued, that once *every year* a secret ballot should be taken among ten non-commissioned officers and older soldiers of ten regiments as to which of the captains would make the best majors, which of the majors the best Lieutenant-Colonels; such a vote would be of use particularly to the authorities when called upon to choose an officer for promotion.

It may be said that officers would be apt in order to secure the vote to be over lenient, to avoid correcting faults etc., but no good officer would do this, and the men would be very quick to recognise the motives of those who do. They would certainly choose the officers who would make the regiments most efficient so far as they could choose between them.

I am thoroughly in accord with you in all your efforts for progress, for the introduction of the useful as opposed to the theatrical. I hold that a vast deal more attention should be given to shooting, and much less time spent upon attaining mechanical precision in obsolete and useless drilling and manoeuvres. I have already I think very much altered the tone of the paper since I have taken it in hand and am ready to go much further, even to the point of advocating promotion above the grade of captain by selection pure and simple directly I see how that selection is to be made so as to be equally fair for men in regiments abroad and at home, with their regiments or in the staff. I shall look with very great interest for the publication of your despatch which will certainly create a great sensation if you state in it the facts you have mentioned to me.

I remain, dear Lord Wolseley
Yours sincerely
G. A. Henty

The following short note, in which he mentions his resignation from the *United Services Gazette* has an envelope which is postmarked 18.12.85.

103 Upper Richmond Road
Putney   Thursday

Dear Lord Wolseley,

I regret that I should have given you the trouble to write twice to me but your kind invitation only reached me on Wednesday morning when I answered at once. It was delayed at the Gazette Office, for owing to a change in the proprietorship of that paper, I retired from the editorship some three months ago, and they stupidly kept the letter three days before forwarding it.

Yours sincerely,
G. A. Henty

The last two letters in the series are simply acceptances of invitations, which make no mention of external events to assist in dateing.

103 Upper Richmond Road
Putney   Monday

Dear Lord Wolseley,

Thanks for your kind letter. I shall have much pleasure in dining with you on Wednesday the 2nd. inst.

Yours very truly
G. A. Henty

Mr Henty has much pleasure in accepting General Viscount
Wolseley's kind invitation for Tuesday next, which only reached
him this morning.
103 Upper Richmond Road
Putney. Dec. 16th.

This series of letters while supplying the bibliographer with a
further title are of obvious importance to the biographer. It is
reasonable to presume that there are similar caches.

To return to his undiscovered printed material, it is known that
he contributed at least one pamphlet for the Boys' Brigade on the
subject of Duty. His connection with this organisation should be
more fully examined. *Chums* for June 26, 1895 states:

Speaking at the Boys' Brigade festival the other night, Mr G. A.
Henty said that he would like boys to be compelled to join the
brigade until they were seventeen, and then to have a year of
camp life. He thought that the discipline was an excellent thing
for boys, and would stop a great deal of the rowdyism and bad
language of the streets.

These address were very often printed by the Brigade and everything points to this as a fruitful area for research.

From the above it would appear that the British collector has a
much better chance of expanding the Henty bibliography than his
American counterpart. Certainly in this country every collector
has an equal chance of finding new Henty items in Readers or
collections of stories but the American collectors would be well
advised to look more closely at the U.S. pirate editions.

Malcolm the Waterboy by D. T. Henty is a highly prized item,
bound in with this is a second Henty 'illegitimate' short story 'On
to Cuba'. 'On to Cuba' is used with the same pagination (pp.
137–209) in what would appear to be the first edition of *The
Golden Cannon* along with 'the Stone Chest or The Secret of
Cedar Island' (Copyrighted, 1896, by the Bright Days Pub. Co.).
None of these three stories are by Henty yet they all appear to be a
deliberate attempt to mislead the public into the belief that they
are his work. 'Malcolm the Waterboy' also first appeared in *Bright
Days*, an American publication for boys and there is every reason
to believe that a search through this publication will unearth other
similar attempts.

These stories are comparatively well known to bibliographers
but other similar examples have been missed:

Bonnie Prince Charlie (*c.* 1917)
Title Page: Bonnie Prince Charlie./A Tale of Fonteney and
   Culloden./By G. A. Henty,/Author (six lines of titles)/illus-

trated by Gordon Browne./M. A. Donohue & Company/Chicago New York/

Cover: grey-green cloth covered boards. Title, author (black). Pictorial card (in black frame) of boy carrying a canoe following an Indian with paddles and baggage along the side of a lake.

Spine: title, author, publisher, decoration of crossed rifles superimposed over an anchor (black).

Contents: 18·2 cm × 11·9 cm. Frontispiece/title page as above/preface, concluded on verso/text: pp (7)–350 (*Bonnie Prince Charlie*) + (87)–99 ('The Balloon-Hoax').

Boards: plain.

Endpapers: white.

Edges: plain.

Catalogue: 5 pp. starting on the verso of the last page of 'The Balloon-Hoax'.

This story also appears in a copy of *The Young Midshipman* (*c*. 1917).

Title Page: The Young Midshipman/A story of/The Bombardment of Alexandria/By/G. A. Henty/Author of (three lines of titles)/flower decoration/Chicago:/M. A. Donohue & Co./

Cover: Light olive-green cloth covered boards. Title, author (dark green). Pictorial card (in dark frame) of Elizabethan Sailors gathered around a mast.

Spine: Title, author, publisher (dark). Decoration of crossed rifles superimposed on an anchor.

Contents: 18·2 cm × 11·9 cm. Frontispiece/title page as above/contents/text: pp. (1)–283 (*The Young Midshipman*) + (87)–99 ('The Balloon Hoax').

Endpapers: white.

Edges: plain

Catalogue: nil.

'The Balloon-Hoax' purports to be the journal of an Atlantic crossing by balloon, one of the central characters is the author Mr Harrison Ainsworth. I have been unable to trace the origin of this story.

Bonnie Prince Charlie (*c*. 1914)

Title Page: Bonnie Prince Charlie./A Tale of Fonteney and Culloden./By G. A. Henty,/Author of (six lines of titles)/Illustrated by Gordon Browne./Chicago:/M. A. Donohue & Co./

Cover: Grey-green cloth covered boards. Title, author, publisher, decoration of boy with sword based on the frontispiece of *Jack Archer*.

Spine: Title, author, publisher, decoration of crossed rifles superimposed over an anchor (dark).

Contents: 10·2 cm × 11·9 cm. Frontispiece/title page as above/preface, concluded on verso/contents, concluded on verso/text: pp. (7)–350 (*Bonnie Prince Charlie*) + (49)–64 ('*William Wilson*').

Endpapers: white.

Edges: plain.

Catalogue: nil.

Several other E. A. Poe stories are used, without acknowledgement, as fillers of *The Queen's Cup* below. This practice is not confined to Henty and one finds the well known 'The Facts in the Case of M. Valdemar' at the end of *Chums of the Camp Fire* by Lawrence Leslie. With an author as well known as Poe there can be no attempt to mislead.

The Queen's Cup (*c.* 1917)

Title Page: The Queen's Cup/A novel/By/G. A. Henty/Chicago/M. A. Donohue & Co./

Cover: Light brown cloth covered boards. Title, author (black). Pictorial card (in black frame) of boy carrying a canoe following an Indian, with paddles and baggage, along the side of a lake.

Spine: Title, author, publisher (black). Decoration of crossed rifles superimposed over an anchor (black).

Contents: 18·1 cm × 11·9 cm. Title page as above, with 'Copyright, 1898, By D. Appleton & Company. *All rights reserved.*' on verso/text: pp. 1–330 (*The Queen's Cup*) + (49)–67 ('William Wilson') + (68)–75 ('Berenice') + (76)–81 ('Eleonora') + (82)–96 ('Ligeia').

Boards: plain.

Endpapers: white.

Edges: plain.

Catalogue: 4 pp. 'Boys' Copyrighted Books'.

All these stories are by E. A. Poe; a less suitable choice for fillers to a novel by Henty could hardly be imagined. One can only wonder if schoolboys buying the book as part of Donohue's Henty series ever took them for the work of their favourite.

The Queen's Cup (*c.* 1918)

Title Page: The Queen's Cup/ a novel/ By/ G. A. Henty/M. A. Donohue & Company/Chicago New York/.

Cover: Light blue cloth covered boards. Title, author (black). Decoration of Viking warrior with axe and shield (black and green), behind his head a panel showing silhouette of a battle scene (green).

Spine: Title, author, publisher (black). Decoration of crossed sword, shield and axe (black and green).

Contents: 10.1 cm. × 11.9 cm. Title page as above, with 'copyright, 1898, By D. Appleton and Company. All rights reserved.' on verso/text: pp. 1–330 (*The Queen's Cup*) + 99–177 ('Blinky Morgan and the Kid').
Boards: plain.
Endpapers: white.
Edges: plain.
Catalogue: 1 p. 'Boys' copyrighted Books' on verso of the last page of text of 'Blinky Morgan and the Kid'.

'Blinky Morgan and the Kid' tells the story of three American safe robbers and murderers. It is obviously American in origin, but as with 'The Balloon–Hoax' I have been unable to trace its source.

Among the Malays (c. 1918)
Title Page: Among Malay Pirates/A Tale of Adventure and Peril/By/G. A. Henty/Author of (three lines of titles)/decoration/M. A. Donohue & Company/Chicago New York/.
Cover: Light blue cloth covered boards. Title, author (black). Decoration of Viking warrior with axe and shield (black and green), behind his head a panel showing silhouette of a battle scene (green).
Spine: Title, author, publisher (black). Decoration of crossed sword, shield and axe (black and green).

Contents: 18.1 cm. × 11.9 cm. Title page as above/contents/text: pp. (1)–274. (*Among Malay Pirates*) + 119–126 ('The Perry Rubber Works').
Boards: plain.
Endpapers: white.
Edges: white.
Catalogue: 2 pp. 'Boys' Copyrighted Books'.

Set in America 'The Perry Rubber Works' tells the story of a swindle and fire at a rubber works. As with the stories above I have been unable to trace the origin of the piece, although it is almost certainly American.

Among the Malays (c. 1914)
Title Page: Among Malay Pirates/A Tale of Adventure and Peril/By/G. A. Henty/Author of (three lines of titles)/decoration/Chicago:/M. A. Donohue & Co./.
Cover: Light green cloth covered boards. Title, author (red-brown). Pictorial card (in red-brown frame) showing prone white men firing at charging natives.
Spine: Title, author, publisher and decoration of crossed rifles superimposed over an anchor (red-brown).
Contents: 18.1 cm. × 12 cm. Frontispiece/title page, as above/contents/text: pp. (1)–274. (*Among Malay Pirates*) + pp. 43–76. ('The Silver Hatchet').

B

Boards: plain.
Endpapers: white.
Edges: plain.
Catalogue: 4 pp.

'The Silver Hatchet' is a sub-Montague Rhodes James story about a weapon used in the Middle Ages for a murder and retaining the power that 'every hand that grasps it be reddened in the blood of a friend'. This story may be English in origin but as with those above the story has not been traced.

Although I have described the format of these items, in every case I have similar copies in the same format which do not contain the additional stories.

It will be noted that the above four items are all published by M. A. Donohue & Co. who also issued some time in the 1890's a 'Fireside Henty Series' (not to be confused with either their 'Fireside Series' or their 'Henty Series'):

Comprising 84 titles by such authors as Henty, Mayne Reid, Baker, Horatio Alger, Oliver Optic, Lover, Defoe, Stowe, Ilsley, Stevenson, etc. Bound in best quality of cloth, stamped on the back and side in ink from a unique and attractive die, and printed on an extra quality of paper from new plates. Olivine edges.   Each book in a printed wrapper.

Cover: Various cloth covered boards. Five panels.
    Top: Horizontal with the words 'Fireside Henty Series', directly underneath this another horizontal panel with a row of shields.
    Two vertical panels:
    Left: Showing a castle on a rock firing cannon.
    Right: A sailing ship returning this fire.
    Bottom: Showing crossed sword and rifle superimposed on ship's steering wheel.
Spine: Vertical row of shields, superimposed over sword. Title, author, publisher.

It will be noted that this is an almost identical binding to that used by both Donohue Bros., and Allison for their 'Henty Series'. The interest in this edition is in the non-Henty titles as one presumes his name still remains on the cover.

Adventures Among the Indians, W. H. G. Kingston; *Adventures in Cuba*, Felix L. Oswald; *Adventures in Tropics*, Fred Gerstacker; *Adventures on Forest and Shore*, Charles Ilsley; *Afloat in the Forest*, Capt. Mayne Reid; *All Aboard*, Oliver Optic; *Among the Malays*, G. A. Henty; *Black Beauty*, Sewall; *Boat Club*, Oliver Optic; *Bonnie Prince Charley* [*sic*], G. A. Henty; *Boy Hunters*, Capt. Mayne Reid;

Boy Knight, The, G. A. Henty; *Bravest of the Brave*, G. A. Henty; *By England's Aid*, G. A. Henty; *By Pike and Dyke*, G. A. Henty; *By Right of Conquest*, G. A. Henty; *By Sheer Pluck*, G. A. Henty; *Buccaneers on Land and Sea*; Capt. Bayley's Heir, G. A. Henty; *Cast up by the Sea*, Sir Samuel W. Baker; *Cat of Bubastes*, G. A. Henty; *Cornet of Horse*, G. A. Henty; *Daniel Boone, Heroes and Hunters of the West*; *Deerslayer*, J. F. Cooper; *Desert Home*, Capt. Mayne Reid; *Dragon and Raven*, G. A. Henty; *Facing Death*, G. A. Henty; *Final Reckoning, A*, G. A. Henty; *For Name and Fame*, G. A. Henty; *Forest and Frontiers*; *For the Temple*, G. A. Henty; *Friends, Though Divided*, G. A. Henty; *Golden Canon*, G. A. Henty; *Handy Andy*, Samuel Lover; *Hero of Pine Ridge*; *Hunting in the Great West*, Shields; *In Freedom's Cause*, G. A. Henty; *In the Reign of Terror*, G. A. Henty; *In Times of Peril*, G. A. Henty; *Jack Archer: A Tale of the Crimea*; *Jack Harkaway's School Days*, Heming; *Last of the Mohicans*, J. F. Cooper; *Lion of St. Mark*, G. A. Henty; *Lion of the North, The*, G. A. Henty; *Lone Ranch, The*, Capt. Mayne Reid; *Maori and Settler*, G. A. Henty; *Mysterious Island*, Jules Verne; *Now or Never*, Oliver Optic; *Ocean Rover*; *One of the 28th*, G. A. Henty; *Orange and Green: A Tale of the Boyne and Limerick*, G. A. Henty; *Out on the Pampas*, G. A. Henty; *Pathfinder*, J. F. Cooper; *Pilot*, J. F. Cooper; *Pioneers*, J. F. Cooper; *Poor and Proud*, Oliver Optic; *Prairie*, J. F. Cooper; *Rangers and Regulators*, Capt. Mayne Reid; *Red Rover*, J. F. Cooper; *Robinson Crusoe*, Defoe; *Scalp Hunters and Rifle Rangers*, Reid; *Slow and Sure*, Horatio Alger; *Spy*, J. Fenimore Cooper; *St. George for England*, G. A. Henty; *Sturdy and Strong*, G. A. Henty; *Through the Fray*, G. A. Henty; *Treasure Island*, R. L. Stevenson; *Try Again*, Oliver Optic; *True to the Old Flag*, G. A. Henty; *Two Admirals*, J. F. Cooper; *Uncle Tom's Cabin*, Stowe; *Under Drake's Flag*, G. A. Henty; *Voyages and Ventures of Famous Sailors. Water Witch*, J. F. Cooper; *Wing and Wing*, J. F. Cooper; *With Clive in India*, G. A. Henty; *With Lee in Virginia*, G. A. Henty; *With Wolfe in Canada*, G. A. Henty; *Wood Rangers; or, The Trappers of Sonora*, Capt. Mayne Reid; *Young Buglers, The*, G. A. Henty; *Young Carthaginians*, G. A. Henty; *Young Colonists, The*, G. A. Henty; *Young Franc-Tireurs*, G. A. Henty; *Young Midshipman*, G. A. Henty.

I have been unable to trace any of the non-Henty items in this series. The above information being copied from the verso of the title page of an M. A. Donohue edition of *Rujub the Juggler* in a different format. I am particularly interested in the seven anonymous titles given below:

Daniel Boone, Heroes and Hunters of the West; Forest and Frontier; Jack Archer: A Tale of the Crimea; Buccaneers on Land and

Sea; Hero of Pine Ridge; Ocean Rover; Voyage and Ventures of Famous Sailors.

The fact that *Jack Archer* is advertised as anonymous casts a doubt as to whether there is or is not an author on the title page of these other works. *Daniel Boone, Heroes and Hunters of the West* may well be credited to Daniel Boone himself. However *Forest and Frontier* has already been noted on page 60 of Dartt's *Bibliography* as a Henty 'illegitimate', although the copy inspected by him, at Indiana, was not in the 'Fireside Henty Series'. It seems more than likely that the other five titles were also issued with the implication that they were by Henty.

The above are not only interesting as 'illegitimates' but in another way which seems to have escaped the attention of American collectors. If the stories of other authors were used as fillers in Henty's books it is more than likely that some of Henty's short stories were regularly used as fillers in the work of other authors. Indeed at least two Federal Book Company editions of *The Lost Heir* use 'A Fishwife's Dream' as a filler.

The only known use of a Henty story as a filler in a work by another author is the reprint edition of *Lone Wolf Cave* by Edward S. Ellis, Donohue *c*. 1919. This edition has been reported as having an olive green cover, there is a fox's head in the centre of the spine. The cover decoration shows two young men with rifles riding amongst rocks and trees. Some editions in this format include twenty-six extra pages of an 'anonymous' story 'Bears and Dacoits. A Tale of the Ghauts.' I have not personally inspected this edition but I accept the description as accurate, thus *Lone Wolf Cave* should be added to the complete bibliography.

The American pirate editions are often careless in their use of Henty illustrations, for example the frontispiece *The Boy Knight*, 'For God and King' illustrates p. 22 of *Friends, Though Divided*. On occasion familiar Henty illustrations are used as a pictorial card to decorate the covers of other titles, as for example, an M. A. Donohue edition of *One of the 28th* (*c*. 1918 identical in format to the second *Bonnie Prince Charlie* described above), both have a coloured pictorial card based on the frontispiece of *Jack Archer*: 'Harry Archer struggled on with his company'; a similar example is a Federal Book Company Edition of *Through the Fray*, which has a coloured pictoral card on the cover based on the Gordon Browne illustration to *With Wolfe In Canada* 'The sergeant told him stories of his travels and adventures'. (p. 54). It is more than likely that these cover designs are repeated on books by other authors.

America and the United Kingdom are not the only countries

where further Henty discoveries can be made. Dartt notes on p. 70 of his *Bibliography*:

BELGRAVIA

The bound volume of an illustrated London magazine, containing a story by 'E. A. Henty'. The Rev. A. B. E. Browne, Camborne, England, is of the definite opinion that this story was not by G. A. Henty, nor does inspection of it reveal any similarity to the writing style of G. A. H.

In fact the story is by E. A. Starkey the wife of Ernest C. Henty with whom she collaborated on *Australian Idylls and Bush Rhymes*. The Australian Hentys are descended from one of the most famous pioneer families who are credited with introducing the Merino sheep to Australia. Henty and his son Charles maintained contact with the Australian branch of the family and although Henty himself never visited Australia his Australian books are packed with authentic detail of that country with which he was presumably supplied by the Melbourne branch of the family. Charles Gerald visited Australia in either 1901 or 1902 when he was convalescing from rheumatic fever which he had contracted during his service with the London Irish Rifles in the Boer War. He married his wife after months of illness and they took a trip round the world staying with some of the Henty family in Melbourne. Frank Henty of the Australian branch wrote at least one book, *The Girl at Blue Creek* under the pseudonym George Checkley presumably so as to avoid confusion with his famous namesake.

There seems to be no connection between G. A. Henty and the William Henty who wrote *Shakespeare, with some notes on his early biography and an identification of the characters William Fenton and Anne Page*. This work was printed in London in 1882 at the Ballantyne Press for private circulation. That Henty's son C. G. Henty wrote for boys is certain. His daughter stated in a letter:

My father did write a few short stories for boys. He was not at all pleased with them and though they were printed he never kept any copies of the journals in which they appeared.

One of these 'Out with the Kimberley Horse' is bound in with Henty's own copy of *Seaside Maidens* (Indiana Collection). Another possible story by him is included in *Storyland for Boys* edited by John England and published by Frederick Warne & Co. Ltd (my copy inscribed 'Xmas 1937'). The story on pp. 106–117 is titled 'Billy Boyce's Big Ears' by C. Henty. It is set in Australia and deals with the recovery of stolen pearls by three boys. The Australian setting could indicate authorship by one of the

Australian Hentys, as Charles Henty according to his daughter always signed himself 'C. G. Henty' but his authorship cannot be ruled out.

It is sad that so little remains that was part of Henty's life. A collection of letters has been tracked to earth but at present the owner, a Mr Karl Huson, is reluctant to allow them to be examined. Mr Huson is I believe a descendant of Mr Henty and as it seems that these papers deal among other things with Hubert Henty's unhappy dealings with the Capital and Counties Bank, and his father's involvement with Andreas Holtz and the Lake Superior Copper Mining Co., two less happy episodes in Henty's life it is his privilege to keep them private. This cannot be the only such hoard. Henty was a well known figure and in an age when people tended to keep letters his are likely to have been especially preserved. Personal items are still coming to light. I recently purchased two water colour seascapes both 25 cm × 36 cm and signed 'G. Henty'. They are hardly inspired masterpieces but they are competently executed.

There is a fair amount of evidence, that Henty was interested in drawing. Fenn's biography states on pp. 26–27:

> . . . not only the pen, but the pencil had become familiar to his fingers, and possibly to fill up dull moments, he began to make sketches of such objects as took his attention; and the idea striking him that such subjects might prove attractive to one of the editors of an illustrated paper at home, he from time to time tried his hand at some little scene or some quaint looking character which had caught his eye . . . . The sketches were duly taken by their recipient to the different London illustrated papers, but whether from not being up to the editorial artistic mark, or from the fact that each paper was already fully represented, no success attended their presentation.

This statement would seem to be confirmed by his grandaughter:

> I think your water colours may well be by G. A. Henty. I'm sure he did enjoy sketching and I *think* especially seascapes from what I remember my father saying. I've never heard of another 'G. Henty' – but again I've never heard of his leaving the 'A' out of his signature. He may well have done so occasionally. All things considered, I feel that it is most likely your pictures are his work, but I'm afraid I don't know how to prove it finally.

My own conviction is that Henty's personal interests are harped on in his work. If these paintings were his work we should expect to find one or more of his heroes displaying a talent for sketching. In *By Right of Conquest* pp. 146–147, we find the hero, Roger

Hawkshaw, explaining the differences between Mexican and European dress to his Mexican hosts by means of sketches:

> He was soon furnished with paper, pens, brushes, and paint; and he drew them several sketches, showing ladies in European fashions, which filled his companions with surprise. It seemed to them impossible that a woman could move with ease and comfort in so much clothing. Then he drew for them a noble in the court dress of the period, and also the figure of a knight in full armour.

These paintings were to be the means of saving Roger's life and later in the same book, pp. 160–164, the theme is enlarged upon:

> 'At one time it seemed to me that the decision would go against you, on the ground that had you been a supernatural being you would have had new arts to teach the people. Fortunately, I had brought with me the pictures you made for my wife and sister, and these I showed them. I pointed out that they were altogether different from the work of our own scribes; that these drew stiff images that looked like representations, not of men and animals, but of wooden creatures, while in your drawings it seemed as if the men and animals were moving across the paper; and that were you to teach our scribes thus to portray objects it would make a profound alteration in Mexican art.'
>
> 'This made a great impression upon them. Many of the nobles belonging to the Council of Education were present, and Montezuma himself is fond of art; all were greatly struck with your paintings, and these certainly went a long way towards strengthening my party. When we get back you shall do some pictures of things such as they see here, and are accustomed to. Perhaps you could do even better still if you were to try.'
>
> 'I could make much more finished pictures,' Roger said; 'these were only sketched off in haste, and with such colours as come to hand; but if I had pigments, and could mix the colours as I wanted them, I could produce very much better effect.'

The text goes on to explain how Roger, as a child had been taught to read and write at a monastery. He had demonstrated a fondness for painting which had been encouraged by the monks. He had continued to sketch while on board ship:

> . . . and had excited a great deal of attention on the part of the friends and acquaintances of Master Diggory Beggs.
>
> Upon his return to Tezcuco, Cacama ordered the scribes to furnish him with large sheets of the best paper, brushes and pigments. The colours were all bright and glaring ones; but by mixing them and adding some sombre dyes he obtained in the market, Roger succeeded in getting the required tints. Taking his place in the garden, at a point where he commanded the lake

near at hand, dotted with canoes, and the city of Mexico, with its
background of hills, in the distance, Roger set to work. To the
surprise of the scribe who had been ordered to assist him, he
mixed the colours with oil instead of water, and then began his
picture. He worked as long as there was sufficient light, and
recommenced it the next morning directly after sunrise, and
continued at work all day, and by evening had finished the picture, three feet by two, which although it would not be considered remarkable in Europe, excited the most lively admiration on the part of Cocama and the ladies. He explained to the
King that as he had none of the spirit that was used in conjunc-
tion with the oil to make it dry rapidly it would be some days
before the picture would be sufficiently dry to be touched.

However the painting is conveyed to Montezuma who presents
Roger with a gold cup and orders him to instruct the Mexican
scribes in this new style of art:

. . . Some attendants were told off to mix colours under his
directions, and to purchase for him in the market all kinds of
dyes and colours he might require.
    A male and female slave, were, at Roger's request, placed at
his service, to act as models; and the attendants had orders to
fetch from the cages and aviaries any beasts and birds he might
desire to copy. Roger had at first some difficulty in preserving
his gravity at this undertaking charge of an art school. At first he
confined himself to sketching from models with a burnt stick on
the white paper, and in seeing that his pupils did the same. Their
drawings had hitherto been purely conventional; they had
always drawn a man in a certain way, not because they saw him
so, but because that was the way in which they had been taught
to draw him; and he had great difficulty in getting them to
depart altogether from these lines and to draw the model exactly
as he stood before them.

In the long passage quoted above Henty shows familiarity with
the needs of an artist. It is not unparalleled in the rest of his work.
In *Facing Death* chapter III, the hero Jack Simpson spends some
time with a painter and in *A Woman of the Commune*, the hero,
Cuthbert Hartington shows great talent as an artist but 'lacked the
application and industry to convert the sketches into finished
paintings' again there is considerable evidence that Henty was
familiar from his own experience with the problems of the artist.
    The main barrier to the acceptance of these paintings as the
work of Henty is the signature 'G. Henty'. I am assured by artists
that there is no relationship between a man's signature with a
brush and with a pen. I therefore, am inclined to believe my water
colours to be the work of G. A. Henty.

This introduction is designed to inspire fellow collectors to make discoveries for themselves. Several previously unrecorded Henty titles have been mentioned above, other obvious omissions from the *Bibliography* include: –

The Reign of Terror (c. 1890)
(The plain binding is the only guide to the date of this title. In the early '90's competition in the American book trade led to more ornamental bindings.) This is Caldwell's version of *In the Reign of Terror*.

Title Page: Shiny paper (as frontispiece). Leaf design (white on brown, 14 cm × 9.5 cm) inside this solid panel of design, placed slightly towards the top left is a white panel (5.8 cm × 10.1 cm), the lettering is on this white panel:
The Reign/of Terror/(leaf)/G. A. Henty/device of hand holding a torch above an open book, underneath this the motto 'Sapere Aude'/H M (two leaves)/Caldwell/Company/New York/

Cover: Olive-green cloth covered boards. No lettering or decoration.

Spine: 'The Reign of Terror' (gold), author (gold), 'Standard Edition' (gold).

Contents: 12.5 cm × 18.6 cm. Frontispiece (portrait of Marat, this is the only illustration)/title page, as above/preface/contents/text (with running title 'In the Reign of Terror'): pp. (1)–321.

Boards: plain.

Edges: plain.

Endpapers: white.

Catalogue: nil.

or

Title Page: As above.

Cover: Olive green cloth. Centre: coat of arms embossed in gold with red cross in centre; behind the coat of arms is a gold embossed verticle sword; draped around the coat of arms and sword is a banner with the words 'Excutcheon/Series' in gold. Corners: a small gold shield with red cross appears in each of the four corners.

Spine: Top: The Reign/of/Terror/line/Henty (all in gold). Middle: Coat of arms and sword design in gold similar to cover, draped with banner that is part in gold and part in red. The words 'Escutcheon/Series'/Illustrated/appears in gold against the red portion of the banner. Bottom: publishers device, then H. M. Caldwell/Company/all in gold.

Contents: Frontispiece (18th-century aristocrat holding bouquet of flowers – not identified)/title page, as above/Preface/contents/Portrait of Marat/text with running title 'In the Reign of Terror'/pp (1) – 321. Other illustrations appear

opposite pages 77 (Marie Antoinette), 132 ('Drunken Women from Paris'), and 238 (Cathedral of Nantes).
Edges: top gilt, others plain
End papers: White
Catalogue: nil

There is no precedence between the two editions, the second presumably being issued at a greater price.

Carne's Hold (c. 1907)
Title Page: The Curse of/Carne's Hold/A Tale of Adventure/By/G. A. Henty/New Edition/Griffith Farran Browne & Co. Limited/35 Bow Street, Covent Garden/London/.
Cover: Red cloth-covered boards. Centre panel showing boy in cap and blazer sitting on a sea wall looking out at a sailing boat and a steam ship, a book is open on his lap (green, grey, red, black and white). Title 'Carne's Hold' (gold contained in panel outlined in green). Author (gold contained in panel outlined in grey).
Spine: Title 'Carne's Hold' (gold). Author (black on green panel). Rose design (green and black). Publisher (black on grey).
Contents: 12.8 cm × 19 cm. Half title/frontispiece/title page as above, on verso 'The Rights of Translation and of Reproduction are reserved.'/contents, concluded on verso/Text: pp. (5)–356.
Boards: plain.
Edges: plain.
Endpapers: white.
Catalogue: nil.

NOTE: The claim of these books to being entered as new titles rests on the rule where by *Among the Malays* is classed as a separate title to *Among Malay Pirates* because it has a variant cover title, although the title page of both items gives the title as *Among Malay Pirates*.

Brave and True (before 1917)
(The date of this book is uncertain. My (a) copy, in paper wrappers, is inscribed 'New Year's Day 1918'. My (b) copy, in paper covered boards, 'Feb. 22nd. 1919' indicating a 1917 publication in wrappers, i.e. during the First World War, and a 1918 publication in boards.)
Title Page: The first letters of 'Brave and True' are red and ornamented (the rest of the lettering is black). The decoration is also in red and black, a much darker red being used for copy (a) in wrappers, this is also true of the first endpaper: Brave & True/Edited by Herbert Strang/Decoration of a castaway on a desert island/London:/Henry Frowde and Hodder & Stoughton/.

Cover: (a) green paper-covered wrappers with pictorial card showing Civil War cavalry charge. 'Edited by Herbert Strang' and title (both white outlined in black).
(b) pink paper-covered boards, then as above.
Spine: (a) plain pink cloth strip.
(b) pink cloth, with title vertically lettered in black.
Contents: (a) 17.7 cm × 22.5 cm. (b) 17 cm × 22 cm. Coloured frontispiece (a) as card on cover (b) illustrating the incident on p. (6) 'Trapped'/title page as above with on verso (a) 'Uniform with this volume' and a note from the editor (b) the note from the editor alone/Text: pp. (1)–(94). All pages unnumbered. (a) two colour plates including frontispiece (b) three colour plates including frontispiece. Henty's contribution, 'Trapped: A tale of the Mexican War' is on pp. (1)–(27). This is taken from *Out on the Pampas*. *Brave & True* is a shortened version of *The Red Book for Boys* which contains the same story.
Boards: plain.
Edges: plain.
Endpapers: white: first endpaper decorated with a sketch of Arabs on board a dhow and a 'This book belongs to . . .' panel (red and black). There is no second front endpaper, that which contains the sketch being glued directly into the spine of the book.
Catalogue: (a) as described on verso of title page
(b) nil.

Fact and Fiction, this small green Macmillan's reading book was published at least four times, 1936, 1937, 1940, 1945. The Henty story is in the section on History pp. 73–84 and is entitled 'A Tight Corner' (from *The Young Carthaginian*). The notes, on page 254, contain a short biographical sketch of Henty together with an explanation of the meaning of certain words. The suggested essay question on page 276 is:

'Describe an adventure with wolves, or among tribesmen.'

The information contained in this introduction is on the whole, speculative or lacking in order. I place it before you as an introduction to Henty collecting and as an indication of some of the areas in which discoveries can be made. There are many other clues still to be pursued, for example Henty's connections with the Ferranti family. It would appear that Charles was in business with Ferranti in the late 1890's and their electrical firm was still in existence after the First World War.

Henty is a jig saw puzzle, a never ending source of surprises, perhaps were the picture clearer the fascination might be less.

Section I

A Guide to the American Editions

In the Introduction to *Hentyana* I particularly listed some of the binding variations to be found in the unofficial American printings. As this list was based on a sample of just over 200 books I did not feel justified in giving approximate dates or placing these editions in any order of precedence. I now possess a holding of just over 1,000 of these unofficial printings and therefore feel justified in revising my introductory list and presenting the following guide to the various American formats.

W. L. ALLISON

Dartt gives the address of this company as Boston, Massachusetts, going on to state that they were important in the publication of cheap cloth-bound books during the latter part of the 1880's.

All my copies seem to be towards the end of the 1890's and the beginning of the 1900's. The company's address is always given as New York.

Binding A 'Fireside Series for Boys' (*c.* 1898)
Cover: Various cloth covered boards. Decoration of crossed rifles and crossed oars, a globe at the intersection between the oars framed in a laurel wreath (black and red). Lettering 'Fireside Series for Boys' (black and red).
Spine: Decoration similar to cover (red and black) title, publisher (black).
Address on Title Page: W. L. Allison Company,/New York./

Binding B '*Henty Series*' (*c.* 1900)
Cover: Four panels, two horizontal top and bottom two vertical centre.
Top panel: 'Henty Series' above a row of shields.
Left centre panel: Sailing Ship.
Right centre panel: A gun battery and a castle on a cliff.

> Bottom panel: Crossed rifle and sword over a ships steering wheel.
> Spine: Title, publisher (gold). Author (red). Decoration of sword and vertical line of shields.
> Address on Title Page: Either/W. L. Allison Company,/New York./or New York/Wm. L. Allison Co./publishers./

This edition advertises 'The Fireside Series for Boys' possibly in the format described above at 50c. The paper for this format is above average with olivine edges and as the almost identical 'Fireside Henty Series' mentioned in the Introduction was priced at 50c, I suspect this was also the price of this edition.

> *Binding C*   'Fireside Series' (*c*. 1901).
> > Cover: Two horizontal panels top and bottom. Three vertical panels centre.
> > Top panel: Head and shoulders of six soldiers and a horse.
> > Left centre panel: Sailor with a rope.
> > Centre panel: Ship sailing up to a castle.
> > Right centre panel: Soldier with a gun over his shoulder.
> > Botton panel: 'Fireside Series', (two tones of one colour used for the decoration and lettering).
> > Spine: Title, author, publisher (in darker tone).
> > Decoration of sailing ship and three seagulls.
> > Address on Title Page: W. L. Allison./New York./

It should be noted that all these Allison bindings are repeated by either M. A. Donohue & Co. or Donohue Bros.

D. APPLETON & CO., New York

I have no examples of 'pirate' editions from this publishing house. They definitely issued the following Henty's *The Art of Authorship* 1890; *Fifty-two Stories for Boys* 1905; and what appears to be the first American edition of *The Queen's Cup* 1898 (No. 246 of Appleton's Town and Country Library). The verso of the title page of pirate editions of *The Queen's Cup* state 'Copyright, 1898, by D. Appleton and Company'. This seems to indicate that Appleton were one of Henty's official American publishers and did not pirate his work.

Fifty-two stories for Boys 1919
> Cover: Grey cloth. Title lettered in red. Black and red decoration, a boy sits on an ornamental frame reading a book. Through the frame can be seen ships, castles, cowboys and soldiers.
> Spine: Title, editor, publisher lettered in red. Device of an open book (black).
> Address on Title Page: D. Appleton and Company/New York/1919

AUXILIARY EDUCATIONAL LEAGUE, Chicago

The 1934 (4th Edition) of *A Book of Famous Travels* volume XII in 'Young Folks' Library' was published by this house.

THE BOOK SUPPLY CO., Chicago

Binding A 'The Peerless Library' (*c*. 1895)
Cover: Plain dark red cloth-covered boards with a ribbed finish.
Spine: Gold bands top and bottom. 'The Peerless Library', title author, publisher (gold).
Address on Title Page: The Book Supply Company,/Publishers,/Chicago,/Ill./.

CHARLES E. BROWN, Boston, Massachusetts

To my knowledge this house only produced Henty's *The Fall of Sebastopol* (1892). *Fighting the Saracens* (1892), and *The Young Buglers* (1892) *The Young Colonists* (1892). These would seem to have been taken over from Roberts Brothers, also of Boston, Massachusetts, who had published *Jack Archer* twice in 1884, the first time under its original title and again as *The Fall of Sebastopol* in what seems to be an official edition by agreement with Henty. They had also published *The Boy Knight* and *Fighting the Saracens* (both the titles identical with *Winning His Spurs* in 1883) in similar formats. There is no reason to suppose that Brown were part of the 'pirate' industry. For purposes of comparison I include a description of the cover of *The Fall of Sebastopol*.

Cover: Bright ochre cloth-covered boards.
Title, author (gold).
Decoration of boy with sword, based on the familiar *Jack Archer* frontpiece but with the background of a ship replacing the battle scene (gold).
All enclosed in black frame.
Rear-cover: Black frame.
Spine: Title, author and sailor stroking his beard (gold).
Address on Title Page: Boston:/Charles E. Brown,/publisher/

All the titles listed above were published in 'The Roundabout Books' *c*. 1892.

Cover: Glazed pictorial boards illustrating the title.
The Young Colonists: A mounted redcoat thrusting his sword through a Zulu warrior's shield.
The Fall of Sebastopol: Kneeling redcoats in bearskin hats,
Fighting the Saracens: Central figure a mounted crusader waving his sword in the air.
The Young Buglers: A line of advancing redcoats with Shako helmets of the Napoleonic war period. A bugler stands just to the rear of them.

Rear Cover: Glazed pictorial board. A globe, flags and
    illustrations of the covers of other titles in the series.
Spine: Red cloth. Title, publisher (black). Decoration
    shows figure carring flag from castle battlements, identi-
    cal with illustration on p. 32 of the first edition of *Win-
    ning of His Spurs.*
Address in Title Page: Boston,/Charles E. Brown & Co./

A. L. BURT, New York

A. L. Burt founded his publishing business in 1887, in 1902 he
incorporated the A. L. Burt Company to include his three sons.

Binding A   (*c*. 1895).
Cover:. Plain dark red cloth-covered boards with a ribbed
    finish.
Spine: Gold bands and leaf decoration top and bottom.
    Title, author, publisher (gold).
Address on Title Page: New York:/A. L. Burt, Publisher./

Binding B   'The Henty Series for Boys' (*c*. 1896).
Cover: Embossed cloth-covered boards.
    Title and author (red).
    Panel above author: Sailor steering a ship.
    Panel below author: Battle scene with five prominent figures
    with swords and rifles, three figures in the background.
Spine: Title (cover colour on gold panel).
    Author, publisher (cover colour on red panels).
    Decoration of an Elizabethan figure with sword in hand and
    two pistols in belt.
Address on Title Page: New York:/A. L. Burt, Publisher./

This edition was priced at $1. It had decorated endpapers but plain
edges.

Binding C   'The Henty Series for Boys' (*c*. 1899).
Cover: Above title panel: A boy in an Eton collar reading by
    an oil lamp.
    Three vertical panels below title.
    Left panel: Sailor with boarding pike.
    Right panel: Eighteenth-century soldier with fire-arm.
    Centre panel: Two Viking ships.
Spine: Author, publisher (red).
    Title (cover colour on gold panel).
    Decoration of two circles.
    Top: A ship.
    Bottom: A fort.
Address on Title Page: Either/New York:/A. L. Burt, Pub-
    lisher./ or A. L. Burt Company, Publishers,/52-58 Duane
    Street, New York./

This edition also priced at $1 seems to have replaced binding B described above. It has plain endpapers but Olivine edges.

Binding D (c. 1899).
Cover: Author, title, 'illustrated' (black).
   Right hand side: Figure of soldier with rifle.
   Left hand side: Floral decoration.
Spine: Title (silver).
   Author, publisher (black).
   Floral Design as on cover.
Address on Title Page: New York:/A. L. Burt, Publisher./

This would appear to be a cheaper edition contemporary with Binding C, above.

Binding E 'The Ideal Series' (c. 1902).
Cover: Title, author (black).
   Decoration of red coated soldier kneeling firing at three just visible over a hill.
   Inset panel of the side of a ship with two smoking cannon, in the foreground a rowing boat with four sailors and an officer.
Spine: Title (silver).
   Author, publisher (black).
   Decoration of two rifles and a sword linked by a leaf design.
Address on Title Page: Either/New York/A. L. Burt, Publisher/or A. L. Burt Company, Publishers/52-58 Duane Street, New York./or A. L. Burt Company,/Publishers, New York./

NOTE: This series has a cream paper dust wrapper, with the same design as that on the cover executed in black, except that the title is replaced on the wrapper by 'The Ideal Series for Boys'.

Binding F (c. 1903).
Cover: Red cloth-covered boards.
   Decoration of a sword (black).
   Title superimposed beneath the hilt (black on light green speckled panel, framed in light green and black). Author superimposed towards point (black on light green scroll framed in black).
   Between title and author, hanging wreath (black and light green).
   Top: On either side of the hilt of the sword, two circles (framed in black).
   Right: Head of mediaeval king (black and cover colour against light green).
   Left: Head of British nineteenth-century soldier (black and cover colour against light green).

Spine: Sword, title and author (as on cover).
Publisher (black).
Address on Title Page: A. L. Burt Company, Publishers,/52–58 Duane Street, New York./

This binding is obviously based on the red uniform binding introduced by Scribner in 1902.

Binding G   (*c*. 1909).
Cover: Title, author (black).
Decoration panel showing Indian and soldier lying down watching pirates embark on the beach below.
Spine: Title (silver).
Author, publisher (black).
Decoration black and red lines with reduced panel as on cover.
Address on Title Page: A. L. Burt Company,/Publishers, New York./

H. M. CALDWELL, New York

Only one title seems to have been published by this house *The Reign of Terror* described in the Introduction.

HENRY T. COATES & CO., Philadelphia

This is another company which does not seem to have issued a regular Henty series. There seems to have been some connection between it and the Winston Co., by which it was later absorbed and Patterson & White on whose press some of Coates' books were printed. I have only two examples from this press.

Binding A   (*c*. 1895). (*By Pike and Dyke*).
Cover: Dark green cloth-covered boards no decoration.
Spine: As cover.
Address on Title Page: Philadelphia/Henry T. Coates & Co./

Binding B   (*c*.1895). *The Cornet of Horse*).
Cover: Design of books, fishing rod, gun and baseball superimposed over a scene showing view through the window of a school-room with table in foreground (black, red, white and gold).
Author and title (black).
Spine: Decoration of a cap, hanging on a peg along with school books, below this another book and a baseball.
Title, author (gold).
Publisher (black).
Address on Title Page: Philadelphia:/Henry T. Coates & Co./Publishers./

A feature of this edition are its beautiful coloured endpapers.
Front: Depicting a fishing scene.
Rear: Two boys seated on a window seat reading.

W. B. CONKEY COMPANY, Chicago

Binding A   (*c*. 1900).
Cover: Title (black).
  Background: Officer with sword and pistol gesturing towards some hills.
  Foreground: Stars and stripes and three bayonets. (black and red).
  All enclosed in black frame.
Spine: Title (gold).
  Sailor on the deck of a ship pulling on a rope.
Address on Title Page: W. B. Conkey Co./Chicago/

Binding B   'Oxford Series' (*c*. 1906).
Cover: Dark red cloth-covered boards, undecorated.
Spine: Gold bands.
  Title, author, 'Oxford Series' (gold).
Address on Title Page: Chicago/W. B. Conkey Company/

Binding C   'Varsity Series' (*c*. 1906)
Cover: Title black in black frame (top third). Boy wearing cap and white sweater with star, baseball bat over right shoulder (bottom two thirds).
Spine: Title, author 'varsity series' (black). Same figure as cover standing in front of plate about to pitch.
Address on Title Page: W. B. Conkey Co./Chicago./

The paper of this edition is vastly superior to the general run of U.S. pirate editions. The verso of the title page advertises the following titles in this series: *Bonnie Prince Charlie/The Boy Knight/The Bravest of the Brave/Facing Death/Jack Archer/True to the Old Flag/With Lee in Virginia/With Wolfe in Canada/The Young Buglers/The Young Colonists/*.

On the evidence of identical binding formats there may well be a connection between this company and the Independence Company.

M. A. DONOHUE AND COMPANY, Chicago

Michael A. Donohue had been a Partner in the Chicago firm of bookbinders Cox and Donohue as early as 1861. After the fire of 1871 the firm was replaced by Donohue, Wilson & Henneberry, which later became the publishers Donohue and Henneberry. A judicial action to dissolve the partnership was initiated in 1900 but presumably the differences went unnoticed as the firm continued in business as Donohue Brothers, not becoming M. A. Donohue and Company until Michael Donohue purchased Henneberry's interest early in 1901. No Henty titles published by Donohue and Henneberry have been located except the hybrid title described below.

M. A. Donohue seems to have continued to issue the editions published by Donohue Brothers, while bringing out the same titles in cheaper formats.

Binding A   'Fireside Henty Series' (*c*. 1902).
Cover: Four panels, two horizontal top and bottom, two vertical centre.
  Top panel: 'Fireside Henty Series' above a row of shields.
  Left centre panel: Sailing ship.
  Right centre panel: A gun battery and a castle on a cliff.
  Bottom Panel: Crossed rifle and sword over a ship's steering wheel.
  All enclosed in a black frame.
Spine: Title, publisher (gold).
  A seven branch candlestick above a panel containing a vertical row of shields superimposed over a sword.
Address on Title Page: Chicago:/M. A. Donohue & Co./ 407-429 Dearborn St./

This is a cheaper version of the format already described for Allison Binding B and also used by Donohue Bros.

Binding B   'The Modern Author's Library' (before 1905).
Cover: Light grey paper wrappers.
  Title, author, publisher (red).
  One of the illustrations from the original edition reproduced on cover.
Spine: Title, author, publisher, 'The Modern Author's Library No. . . . . .' (black).
Rear-cover: Advertisements.
Address on Title Page: Chicago:/M. A. Donohue & Co./407–429 Dearborn St./

Binding C   'Henty Series' (*c*. 1905).
Cover   'Henty Series' (black).
  Decoration of booted figure standing with rifle.
  Top, background panel of tiger in jungle setting.
  Right of figure a shield containing a square.
Spine: Title, author, publisher (black).
  Panel decoration: A gun firing at a ship.
Address on Title Page: Chicago:/M. A. Donohue & Co./407–429 Dearborn St./

Binding D (*c*. 1906).
Cover: Title, author (black).
  Decoration of booted figure standing with rifle.
  Top, background panel of tiger in jungle setting.
  Right of figure a shield containing a square.
Spine: Title, author (black).
  Panel decoration: A gun firing at a ship.
Address on Title Page: Chicago:/M. A. Donohue &
Co./407–429 Dearborn St./

Binding E   (*c*. 1908).
Cover: Title, author (black).
  Decoration: Man with rifle and haversack sitting beside a
cannon.
Spine: Title, author, publisher (black).
  Decoration of bugle in panel.
Address on Title Page: Chicago/M. A. Donohue & Com-
pany/407–429 Dearborn Street./

The following series of seven almost identical bindings seem to
date between 1914–1920. The only reason for placing possible
dates against particular pictorial cards is inscriptions on the
endpapers. I do have more than one copy of each of the following
items and in some cases two or three copies of the same title with
different cards, so that it seems reasonable to assume that the
whole series of 45 titles was produced in each of the following
formats.

Binding F   (*c*. 1914) Coloured.
Cover: Title, author (dark).
  Pictorial card of Elizabethan sailors standing around a mast.
Spine: Title, author, publisher (dark).
  Decoration of crossed rifles superimposed on an anchor.
Address on Title Page: Chicago:/M. A. Donohue & Co./

Binding G   (*c*. 1914).
Cover: Title, author (dark).
  Pictorial card of white men lying firing at charging natives.
Spine: Title, author, publisher (dark).
  Decoration of crossed rifles superimposed on an anchor.
Address on Title Page: Chicago:/M. A. Donohue & Co./

Binding H   (*c*. 1914).
Cover: Title, author (dark).
  Pictorial card of European soldiers surrounded by mounted
Indians.
Spine: Title, author, publisher (dark).
  Decoration of crossed rifles superimposed on an anchor.
Address on Title Page: Chicago:/M. A. Donohue & Co./

Binding I   (*c*. 1914).
Cover: Title, author (dark).
   Pictorial card is based on the frontpiece of *Jack Archer*.
Spine: Title, author, publisher (dark).
   Decoration of crossed rifles superimposed on an anchor.
Address on Title Page: Chicago:/M. A. Donohue & Co./

This copy inscribed 1919 advertises only 43 titles as opposed to
the 45 titles advertised in the copies on the previous page.

Binding J   (*c*. 1914).
Cover: Title, author (dark).
   Pictorial card depicts a boy with a revolver lost in a forest.
Spine: Title, author, publisher (dark).
   Decoration of crossed rifles superimposed on an anchor.
Address on Title Page: Chicago:/M. A. Donohue & Co./

Binding K   (*c*. 1917).
Cover: Title, author (dark).
   Pictorial card is a coloured representation of the illustration p.
   276 of *Friends, Though Divided*, 'The Sea Fight.'
Spine: Title, author, publisher (dark).
   Decoration of crossed rifles superimposed on an anchor.
Address on Title Page: M. A. Donohue & Com-
   pany/Chicago/New York/

Binding L   (*c*. 1917).
Cover: Title, author (dark).
   Pictorial card of Elizabethan sailors standing around a mast.
Spine: Title, author, publisher (dark).
   Decoration of crossed rifles superimposed on an anchor.
Address on Title Page: Chicago:/M. A. Donohue & Co./

Binding M   (*c*. 1917).
Cover: Title, author (dark).
   Pictorial card depicts a boy carrying a canoe following an
   American Indian with baggage and paddles.
Spine: Title, author, publisher (dark).
   Decoration of crossed rifles superimposed on an anchor.
Address on Title Page: Chicago:/M. A. Donohue & Co./ or M.
   A. Donohue & Company/Chicago/New York/or Chicago/M.
   A. Donohue & Co/

Binding N   (*c*. 1917).
Cover: Title, author (black).
   Viking warrior with shield and axe three colours used (black
   + 2).
   Behind head a panel showing silhouette of a battle scene.
Spine: Title, author, publisher (black).
   Decoration of Viking, sword, shield and axe (black + 2 col-
   ours).
Address on Title Page: Chicago:/M. A. Donohue & Co./

Binding O (*c*. 1922).
Cover: Title, author (black).
   Viking warrior with shield and axe two colours used (black + one).
   Behind head a panel showing silhouette of a battle scene.
Spine: Title, author, publisher (black).
   Decoration of Viking, sword, shield and axe (black + one colour).
Address on Title Page: Chicago:/M. A. Donohue & Company,/

Binding P (*c*. 1930).
Cover: Title, author (black).
   Viking warrior with shield and axe (black).
Spine: Title, author, publisher (black).
   Decoration of Viking, sword, shield and axe (black).
Address on Title Page: M. A. Donohue & Company/Chicago New York/

DONOHUE BROTHERS, Chicago

As this company was only in existence for a little over a year, succeeding Donohue & Henneberry on April 14, 1900 and being in turn succeeded by M. A. Donohue & Co., on March 30, 1901, all its binding formats must fall between these two dates, although inscriptions on the endpapers indicate that the new company continued to issue the 'Henty Series'.

Binding A (*c*. 1900).
Cover: Decoration of Greek head in winged circle, over a parchment with hanging seals.
Rear-cover: Seal suspended from a tape.
Spine: Title, author (gold).
   Publisher (dark).
   Decoration of hanging seals.
Address on Title Page: Donohue Brothers/Chicago – New York./

Binding B '*Henty Series*' (*c*. 1900).
Cover: Four panels, two horizontal top and bottom two vertical centre.
   Top panel: 'Henty Series' above a row of shields.
   Left centre panel: A Sailing Ship.
   Right centre panel: A gun battery and a castle on a cliff.
   Bottom panel: Crossed rifle and sword over a ship's steering wheel.
Spine: Title, publisher (gold). Author (red).
   Decoration of sword and vertical line of shields.
Address on Title Page: Donohue Brothers/Chicago – New York./

Binding C 'Fireside Series' (*c*. 1901).

Cover: Two horizontal panels top and bottom.
Three vertical panels centre.
Top panel: Head and shoulders of six soldiers and a horse.
Left centre panel: Sailor with a rope.
Centre panel: Ship sailing up to a castle.
Right centre panel: Soldier with a gun over his shoulder.
Bottom panel: 'Fireside Series' (two tones of one colour used for the decoration and lettering).

Spine: Title, author, publisher (in darker tone).
Decoration of sailing ship and three seagulls.

Address on Title Page: Donohue Brothers/Chicago -- New York./

DONOHUE HENNEBERRY & CO., Chicago.

As this company grew out of a bookbinding business it is not surprising that the only Henty so far located should be a hybrid publication of which only the spine carries the name of this house.

Binding A   (*c*. 1895).

Cover: Brown cloth embossed in black as follows: three different horizontal frieze designs occupy the top third of the cover; the same designs are repeated in reverse order in the bottom third; the centre is occupied by a still different horizontal design with a circle in the centre.

Spine: Top: black embossed design/horizontal black line/title and author in gold/horizontal black line/another black design/Donohue/Henneberry/& Co. (in black) another design in black at bottom.

Address on Title Page: New York/Worthington Company/747 Broadway/or New York,/Worthington Co, 747 Broadway,/1890,/or New York/Worthington Company, 747 Broadway/1890/

End papers: Yellow and cream pebble design.

This would appear to be a late remainder issue from the Worthington plates. Note that although the title pages refer to illustrations, there are no illustrations used.

E. P. DUTTON & COMPANY, New York

This company should not be considered along with the unofficial U.S. publishers. It only issued the Henty titles published by Griffith and Farran and Griffith, Farran, Okeden & Welsh. The address on the title page reading:

1882   (a) Griffith and Farran,
Successors to Newbery and Harris,
Corner of St. Paul's Churchyard, London.
E. P. Dutton & Co., New York.

1833   (b) Griffith and Farran,
           Successors to Newbery & Harris,
           West Corner of St. Paul's Churchyard, London.
           E. P. Dutton & Co., New York.

1884   (c) Griffith and Farran,
           (Successors to Newbery & Harris,)
           West Corner of St. Paul's Churchyard, London.
           E. P. Dutton & Co., New York.

The above addresses were all copied from Griffith and Farran editions. *Out on the Pampas* exists in an edition with the (b) title page address, with an 1882 dated Dutton catalogue and 'Dutton & Co.' on the spine. The format is similar to Griffith & Farran's 'Boys' Own Favourite Library' with a cover design of a boy sitting halfway up a tree reading a book. 'Boys' Own Favourite Series' replaces 'Boys' Own Favourite Library' and the gold panel with the title and author is placed at an angle instead of being parallel to the top of the book.

A much later Dutton binding format issued in 1893 was still being printed by Morrison & Gill of Edinburgh with a tipped in title page:

    Cover: Red cloth-covered boards. 'Boys' (cover colour on black banner) 'Favorite Series' (gold). Green wreath centre. Foot of cover, five stars (four gold, one black).
    Spine: Wreath and banner decoration similar to cover. Stars (black). Title (cover colour on gold panel). Author, publisher (gold).
    Address on Title Page: New York/E. P. Dutton & Company/31 West Twenty-Third Street/

It would seem from the above that this company was among the first to import Henty's into America, in the early 80's and are possibly a more significant U.S. publisher than Scribner.

EDUCATIONAL PUBLISHING COMPANY, Boston

I have traced only one Henty from this house, this is what appears to be the official American printing of *Tales from Henty* (*c.* 1895). For purposes of comparison I include a description of the cover:

    Cover: Light brown cloth-covered boards. Two axes and a spear joined by a ribbon and a laurel wreath (dark brown). From the spear a pennant with the motto 'Tales' underneath 'From Henty' (dark brown).
    All enclosed in double line frame (dark brown).
    Spine: Title lettered vertically (dark brown).
    Address on Title Page: Educational Publishing Company,/Boston New York Chicago San Francisco/

EXCELSIOR PUBLISHING HOUSE, New York.

(Several Henty's were published by this house. I have been unable to locate copies for inspection.)

FARRAR AND RINEHART INCORPORATED, New York

This house published *Famous Stories of Five Centuries,* (1934). This was the U.S. edition of *Gateway of Literature*. The American title would seem to derive from the dust wrapper of the British edition where it is used in preference to *Gateway of Literature*.

FEDERAL BOOK COMPANY, New York

As this company did not come into existence until 1902, being identical with the F. M. Lupton publishing Company, no formats exist before this date.

> *Binding A   c.* 1902 (this format inherited from Lupton)
> Cover: Title, author (black).
>   Panel above title: Two daggers, crossed rifles and a laurel wreath.
>   Large panel, below title, containing two smaller oval panels:
>   Right: Sea battle with rowing boat in foreground, and monogram W F.
>   Left: General and staff on horseback watching infantry battle.
>   Between the ovals stars and stripes shield, cannon, ramrod and cannon balls.
> Spine: Title (gold).
>   Author, publisher (black).
>   Decoration of crossed swords and laurel wreath.
> Address on Title Page: New York:/The F. M. Lupton publishing Company,/

> *Binding B   c.* 1902.
> Cover: Title, author (black).
>   Panel above title: Two daggers, crossed rifles and a laurel wreath.
>   Large panel, below title, containing two smaller oval panels:
>   Right: Sea battle with rowing boat in foreground, and monogram W F.
>   Left: General and staff on horseback watching infantry battle.
>   Between the ovals stars and stripes shield, cannon, ramrod and cannon balls.
> Spine: Title (gold).
>   Author, publisher (black).
>   Decoration of crossed swords and laurel wreath.
> Address on Title Page: New York/The Federal Book Company/Publishers/

Binding C   c. 1903.
Cover: Title, author (black).
   Panel above title: Lakeside scene with two boats.
   Panel below title: Pictorial card (This coloured card is based
   on the Gordon Browne illustration on p. 54 *With Wolfe in
   Canada* 'The sergeant told him stories of his travels and
   adventures,' although the girl in the background of the origi-
   nal drawing is picking fruit and not listening to the story.) of
   man with raised stick telling a story to a boy, lying on the
   ground and girl holding a doll.
Spine: Title (gold).
   Publisher (black).
   Decoration of skis and snowshoes above tree lined lake with
   two yachts.
Address on Title Page: New York/The Federal Book Com-
   pany/publishers/

Binding D   c. 1903.
Cover: Title, author (black).
   Panel above title: Lakeside scene with two boats.
   Panel below title: Pictorial card depicts white men lying firing
   at charging natives.
Spine: Title (gold).
   Publisher (black).
   Decoration of skis and snowshoes above tree lined lake with
   two yachts.
Address on Title Page: New York and London/Street and
   Smith,/Publishers/

This pictorial card is identical with M. A. Donohue binding F.

Binding E   (c. 1905).
Cover: Author, title (black).
   Decoration of three panels.
   Top panel above title: American eagle with two flags.
   Left hand panel below title: Two sailors aiming a cannon,
   officer in the background looking through field glasses.
   Right hand panel below title: U.S. cavalryman with sabre
   raised to cut down soldier on ground aiming a pistol.
Spine: Author, title, publisher (black).
   Decoration of rifle and American flag.
Address on Title Page: New York/The Federal Book Com-
   pany/Publishers/

R. F. FENNO & COMPANY, New York

Fenno are only known to have published two Henty titles, both
variant titles of the same story and both in 1895: *Two Sieges of
Paris* and *A Girl of the Commune*. These would seem to be by
arrangement with Henty as the verso of the title pages carry the

legend 'Copyright 1895, by G. A. Henty'. For purposes of comparison I include a description of the bindings of two variant editions of *A Girl of the Commune*.

Binding A   (1895).
Cover: Olive green cloth-covered boards.
Decoration of a woman in a long flowing robe holding a spear (red and black). Behind her the silhouette of the Paris skyline (black), with behind that a setting sun (gold with gold rays). Behind the woman's head a label (gold outlined in black), with the title (cover colour outlined in black). Author (gold). At the foot of the cover a plant design (black).
Spine: Title, author, publisher (gold).
Decoration of three spears (black).
Address on Title Page: New York/R. F. Fenno & Company/112 Fifth Avenue/

Binding B   (after 1895).
Cover: Light blue cloth-covered boards.
Title, author (white).
Decoration composed of six circles and plant design (white).
Spine: Circle and plant design similar to cover.
Title, author, publisher (white).
Address on Title Page: New York/R. F. Fenno & Company/9 and 11 East 16th Street/

Two Sieges of Paris (after 1895)
Cover: Title, author (gold). Rapiers and trident superimposed on heraldic lions. Decoration red and blue on grey background.
Spine: Title, author, publisher (gold). Red sword with blue decoration behind the hilt.
Address on Title Page: New York/R. F. Fenno & Company/9 and 11 East 16th Street/

GROSSET AND DUNLAP, New York

Founded in 1900 by A. Grosset of Grosset and Company and George T. Dunlap who is recorded in *The Publisher's Weekly* (21/1/1899) as being about to become a representative on the work for Rand, McNally and Company.

Binding A   1906.
Cover: Three panels contained in a black frame.
Top: Title (black).
Centre: Blue oval containing head and shoulders of naval officer in a greatcoat. On either side, the barrels of two cannons (black). Below, author (black).
Bottom: Scene showing horseman with lariat.

Spine: Title, author, publisher (black).
  Sailing boat in panel above author.
Address on Title Page: New York/Charles Scribner's
  Sons/1906/

The address on the title page would seem to indicate that this
house may have published their Henty's in association with Henty's official publisher, this is further confirmed by the verso of the
title page which states 'Copyright, 1902, By Charles Scribner's
Sons — Published, September, 1902'.

  Binding B (*c.* 1920).
  Cover: Yellow cloth-covered boards.
    Title, sub-title, author (blue).
    Decoration of state sword (blue).
  Dust-wrapper: Red, yellow and white with the frontpiece
    reproduced in colour.
    Rear: Advertisement for 'Famous Tales of Adventure', no
    Henty titles advertised.
  Spine: Title, author, publisher, device (blue).
  Address on Title Page: Grosset & Dunlap/Publishers/New
    York/

The spine is almost identical to that of the Scribner Series for
Young People 1919 onwards and the format would seem to bear
out the comments made on binding A, the type face being identical
with that used by Scribners.

HALL AND LOCKE COMPANY, Boston

This company published the first, second and third editions of *A
Book of Famous Travels* copyright 1901, 1902, cf. Auxiliary Educational League.

HARPER AND BROTHERS, New York and London

The house published only one Henty title *In the Hands of the
Cave-Dwellers*. There is no reason to suppose that this was published without the author's consent. This was published in two
formats which for purposes of comparison are given below:

  Binding A 1900.
  Cover: Dark green cloth-covered boards.
    Decoration of Mexican holding a rifle (tan, orange, white and
    black).
    Title, author (orange).
  Spine: Title, author, publisher (gold).
  Address on Title Page: Harper & Brothers/New York and
    London/1900/

Binding B   1904.
Cover: Cream cloth-covered boards.
   Decoration of boy sitting on a wall reading (red and blue).
   Title, author (red).
Spine: Title, author, publisher (red).
Address on Title Page: New York and London/Harper &
   Brothers Publishers/1904/

GEORGE H. HILL, Chicago.
Founded in 1900 went bankrupt in 1902, connected with the Mershon Co.

Binding A   c. 1900.
Cover: Panel top containing:
   Right: Head and shoulders of an officer (black against red
   background).
   Left: Title (black). Nine daggers (black), within laurel
   wreaths (red). Author (black in red panel).
Spine: Title, author (gold).
   Three daggers (black).
Address on Title Page: Chicago/Geo. H. Hill Co./Publishers/

HURST AND COMPANY, New York
Founded in 1871 by Thomas D. Hurst, it was absorbed by the
Nourse Company in 1924 which was in turn absorbed by the Platt
and Munck Company in 1926. No Edition by either of the two
later houses has been located.

Binding A   (c. 1898).
Cover: Black floral design with eastern lamp in centre.
Spine: Title, author (gold).
   Publisher (black).
   Black ornamentation with winged horse on title page.
Address on Title Page: New York/Hurst & Company/Publishers/

Binding B   (c. 1898).
Cover: Title (black).
   Decoration of leaves and three flowers.
Spine: Title, author (gold).
   Publisher (black).
   Decoration similar to cover.
Address on Title Page: New York:/Hurst & Company/Publishers/
This format is similar in size and quality to binding A and would
seem of approximately the same period.

Binding C   (c. 1898).
Cover: Title (black).

Decoration of leaves and three flowers.
Spine: Title, author (gold).
   Publisher (black).
   Decoration similar to cover.
Address on Title Page: New York/Hurst & Company,/Pub-
   lishers./

Binding D   (*c*. 1899).
Cover: Black panel with leaf decoration (cover colour).
   In centre publisher's monogram (black on green), all outlined
   in green and black flower decoration.
Spine: Decoration similar to cover.
   Title, author (gold). Contained within two decorated gold
   bands.
Address on Title Page: New York/Hurst & Company/Pub-
   lishers/

Binding E   (*c*. 1899).
Cover: Floral *art nouveau* decoration.
Spine: Decoration similar to cover but with gold added.
   Title, author (gold).
Address on Title Page: New York:/Hurst & Company,/ Pub-
   lishers./

Binding F   (*c*. 1901).
Cover: Decoration similar in quality but less ornate than bind-
   ing C.
   Title (black), between two flowers.
Spine: Floral design (some gold).
   Title, author (gold).
   Publisher (black).
Address on Title Page: New York/Hurst and Company/Pub-
   lishers/

Binding G   (*c*. 1901).
Cover: Decoration of six flowers arranged at the top of the
   cover in two rows of three, bottom of cover stems.
Spine: One flower and stems similar to cover (gold).
   Title, author (gold).
   Publisher (black).
Address on Title Page: New York/Hurst and Company/Pub-
   lishers/

Binding H   (*c*. 1901).
Cover: Red cloth-covered boards.
   Five embossed circles centre containing flower, all linked by
   double lines (embossed).
Spine: Title, author (gold, contained in gold leaf decoration).
   Embossed circle containing flower.
   Publisher (embossed).

Address on Title Page: New York/ Hurst and Company/Publishers/

Binding I   (*c*. 1901).
Cover: Red cloth-covered boards.
   Five embossed circles centre containing flower, all linked by double lines (embossed).
Spine: Title, author (gold, contained in gold leaf decoration).
   Embossed circle containing flower.
   Publisher 'Hurst' (embossed).
Address on Title Page: New York/The F. M. Lupton Publishing Company/

Binding J   (*c*. 1901).
Cover: Title, author (black).
   Decoration of blue coated cavalry officer with raised sword, background sky (orange), silhouette of massed cavalry (black), contained in a circle.
Spine: Title (gold).
   Publisher (black).
   Floral device (orange and black).
   Running figure with rifle (blue and orange).
Address on Title Page: New York/Hurst & Company/Publishers/

Binding K   (*c*. 1902).
Cover: Standing figure holding rifle, in the background trees and camp fire.
Spine: Title, author (gold).
   Panel of trees and waterfall.
   Standing figure as on cover.
   Publisher (same colour as figure).
Address on Title Page: New York/Hurst and Company/Publishers/

Binding L   (*c*. 1902).
Cover: Pictorial card of officer waving a sword, he is wearing khaki and riding a black horse (background a circle of red).
   Title, author (black on red).
   Outside circle green leaf design on gold.
Spine: Title (gold).
   Author, publisher 'Hurst & Co.' (black).
   Decoration of sword with laurel wreath behind hilt (black).
Address on Title Page: New York/The Federal Book Company/Publishers/

Binding M   (*c*. 1902).
Cover: Title (black).
   Decoration of two daffodils and small oval pictorial card showing Edwardian Society Lady.
Spine: Title, publisher, daffodil (black).

Address on Title Page: New York/Hurst & Company/Publishers/'

Binding N 'The Hawthorne Library'.
Cover: Yellow paper covered wrappers.
  Title, author, publisher (dark brown).
  Centre: Floral design (brown and dark brown).
Spine: Series, price, author (lettered horizontally, dark brown).
  Title (lettered vertically dark brown).
Address on Title Page: New York:/Hurst and Company,/Publishers./

Binding O Pictorial card dated 1907.
Cover: Pictorial card showing cavalier in red cloak.
  Sword upraised in the right hand, plumed hat in the left.
  Title, author (black).
Spine: Title (gold).
  Author, publisher and figure of cavalier similar to figure on cover but with sword pointed downwards (black).
Address on Title Page: New York/Hurst & Company/Publishers/or New York/Hurst & Company/Publishers./

Binding P (*c*. 1907).
Cover: Author, title (black).
  Pictorial card.
  Smaller panel showing street scene, figure lying dead or wounded.
  Central foreground figure of cavalier with open doublet and drawn sword.
Spine: Title, author (gold).
  Panel of trees and waterfall.
  Standing figure as on cover.
  Publisher (same colour as figure).
Address on Title Page: New York/Hurst & Company/Publishers./

Binding Q 'Henty Series for Boys' (*c*. 1915).
Cover: Pictorial card of mounted redcoat with sword, leading red coated infantry (the background infantry contained in a panel)
  Title, author (dark blue).
Spine: Title (gold).
  Author, publisher, running figure with rifle (dark blue).
Address on Title Page: New York/Hurst & Company/Publisher/

Binding R 'Henty Series for Boys' (*c*. 1915).
Cover: Pictorial card of mounted khaki clad soldier, with sword.
  Background of charging cavalry with U.S. Flag (in panel).

c

Title, author (dark blue).
Spine: Title (gold).
Author, publisher 'Hurst & Co.' (black).
Decoration of sword with laurel wreath behind hilt (black).
Address on Title Page: New York/Hurst & Company/Publishers./

In spite of the slight difference of the fullstop after 'Publishers.' in the address in Binding M, I think these are alternative formats for the same series. There being a choice between a cover with British and a cover with U.S. Soldiers.

Binding S 'Henty Series for Boys' (*c*. 1917).
Cover: Pictorial card of officer waving a sword, he is wearing khaki and riding a black horse (background a circle of red).
Title, author (black on red).
Outside circle green leaf design on gold.
Spine: Title, author, publisher, running figure with rifle (dark blue).
Address on Title Page: New York/The Federal Book Company/Publishers./

Binding T 'Henty Series for Boys' (*c*. 1917).
Cover: Title (black).
Decoration of two daffodils and small oval pictorial card showing Edwardian Society Lady.
Spine: Series, price, author (lettered horizontally, dark brown).
Title (lettered vertically, dark brown).
Address on Title Page: New York/Hurst & Company/Publishers./

This edition has a white dust wrapper with a design similar to cover. It is reasonable to deduce similar dust wrapper for bindings L:M:N:P & Q.

Binding U 'Henty Series for Boys' (*c*. 1919).
Cover: Pictorial card of standing khaki clad soldier with sword in right hand, revolver in left.
In the background gun position and Union Jack.
Title (dark blue).
Author (red).
Spine: Series, price, author (lettered horizontally, dark brown).
Title (lettered vertically, dark brown).
Similar figure as on cover but with sword pointed downwards.
Address on Title Page: New York/Hurst & Company/Publishers./

Binding V 'Henty Series for Boys' (*c*. 1919).
Cover: Pictorial card of khaki clad soldier on white horse in the background military buildings with stars and stripes flag.
Title (dark blue).
Author (red).
Spine: Series, price, author (lettered horizontally, dark brown).
Title (lettered vertically, dark brown).
Publisher (same colour as figure).
Similar figure as on cover but with sword pointed downwards.
Address on Title Page: New York/Hurst & Company/Publishers/

It will be noted that the pictorial card bindings K–P, approximately correspond to the Donohue bindings E–L.

THE INDEPENDENCE COMPANY, Chicago

Binding A (*c*. 1900).
Cover: Title (black).
Background: Officer with sword and pistol gesturing towards some hills.
Foreground: Stars and stripes and three bayonets (black and red).
All enclosed in black frame.
Spine: Title (gold).
Sailor on the deck of a ship pulling on a rope.
Address on Title Page: The Independence Co./Chicago/

INTERNATIONAL BOOK COMPANY, New York

Dartt reports that this company went out of business on March 12, 1892. The fact that among the titles they published *A Tale of Waterloo* suggests a possible connection with the Worthington Company.

Binding A (*c*. 1890).
Cover: Title, crossed rifles, author (silver).
A laurel wreath (dark).
Spine: Title, author, publisher, officer's sword (silver).
Laurel wreath (dark).
Address on Title Page: New York/International Book Company/310–318 Sixth Avenue/

J. B. LIPPINCOTT AND COMPANY, Philadelphia

Dartt states in his *Companion* 'operated under this name after an 1885 name change' yet this house was the American publisher of *The Cornet of Horse* 1881. This edition is identical in every way, save the name of the publisher on the spine and the address on the title page, to the Sampson Low, Marston, Searle and Rivington 1881 edition. On p. (279) it states 'London: Printed by Gilbert and Rivington Limited, St. John's Square'. This is perhaps the first Henty to be imported into America (Cf. E. P. Dutton & Company, above). I find it odd as this house imported *The Cornet of Horse*, that they did not also import *Jack Archer* and *Winning His Spurs* and I would not be surprised to discover editions of these titles by Lippincott. This company also published 1900 *The Brahmin's Treasure* (copyright 1897). There seems no reason to believe that any of these publications were pirated. Address on title page of *The Cornet of Horse*: Philadelphia:/J. B. Lippincott & Co./1888/

Brahmin's Treasure

Binding A   (1900).
Cover: Light brown cloth-covered boards, title, author (red). Decoration of Indian peering round flap of curtain (red and black) on right hand side.
Spine: Title, author, publisher (gold).
Address on Title Page: Philadelphia/J. B. Lippincott Company/1900/

Binding B   1908
Cover: Blue cloth-covered boards. Title and author lettered in dark blue.
Decoration at top of cover shows youth with lantern peering into treasure cave (dark blue and orange).
Spine: Title, author, publisher (dark blue).
Address on Title Page: Philadelphia/J. B. Lippincott Company/1908/

F. F. LOVELL, New York

JOHN W. LOVELL, New York

It will be noted that the bulk of the editions described in this paper date from some time after the passage of the International Copyright Act in March 1891.

F. F. Lovell and J. W. Lovell were brothers running rival companies in the cut-throat era of cheap U.S. publishing (1800–1891). The main Henty publishers during this era were the Lovells, Munro, Taylor, Ogilvie, and Worthington. In 1889 Frank Lovell anticipated the International Copyright Law by beginning to publish 'by arrangement with the authors', while his brother John combined several leading U.S. publishers of cheap reprints into *The United States Book Company* in an attempt to put an end to price cutting.

F. M. LUPTON PUBLISHING COMPANY, New York

Binding A (*c*. 1900).
Cover: Leaf design with torch and laurel wreath top centre (black and green).
Spine: Three panels:
Top: Plant design (green and black), title and author (gold).
Centre: Plant design (gold).
Bottom: Plant design (green and black) beneath this, publisher (black).
Address on Title Page: New York/The F. M. Lupton publishing Company/72–76 Walker Street/

Binding B (*c*. 1900).
Cover: Honey-suckle design with two bees.
W F monogram on left hand side.
Title, author (black) contained in shield panels.
Spine: Title, author (gold).
Publisher (black).
Honey-suckle decoration similar to cover but with some gold added.
Address on Title Page: New York:/The F. M. Lupton Publishing Company./

Binding C (*c*. 1900).
Cover: Author, title (black, inside rectangular panels).
Floral decoration, similar to Binding B but without bees or monogram.
Spine: Author, title (gold).
Publisher (black).
Floral decoration similar to cover but with some gold added.
Address on Title Page: New York:/The F. M. Lupton Publishing Company./

Binding D (*c*. 1900).
Cover: Title, author (black).
Two panels:
Above title: Boy lying on the ground reading a book.
Below title: A soldier and sailor on guard with an iron-clad in the background.
Spine: Title (gold).
Author, publisher (black).
Decoration of figure holding a rifle, trees in the background.
Address on Title Page: New York:/The F. M. Lupton Publishing Company./

Binding E (*c*. 1902).
Cover: Plain dark green cloth-covered boards.
Spine: Title, author (gold).
Contained within two gold bands.

Address on Title Page: New York:/The F. M. Lupton Publishing Company./

Binding F   (*c*. 1901).
Cover: Title, author (black).
   Panel above title: Two daggers, crossed rifles and a laurel wreath.
   Large panel, below title, containing two smaller oval panels:
   Right: Sea battle with rowing boat in foreground, and monogram W F.
   Left: General and staff on horseback watching infantry battle. Between the ovals, stars and stripes shield, cannon, ramrod and cannon balls.
Spine: Title (gold).
   Author, publisher 'F. M. Lupton' (black).
   Decoration of crossed swords and laurel wreaths.
Address on Title Page: New York:/The F. M. Lupton Publishing Company./

Binding G   (*c*. 1902).
Cover: Title, author (black).
   Panel above title: Two daggers, crossed rifles and a laurel wreath.
   Large panel, below title, containing two smaller oval panels:
   Right: Sea battle with rowing boat in foreground, and monogram W F.
   Left: General and staff on horseback watching infantry battle. Between the ovals, stars and stripes shield, cannon, ramrod and cannon balls.
Spine: Title (gold).
   Author, publisher 'The Federal Book Co.' (black).
   Decoration of crossed swords and laurel wreath.
Address on Title Page: New York:/The F. M. Lupton Publishing Company./

The name of this company was changed to Federal Book Company in 1902.

MANHATTAN PUBLISHING COMPANY, New York

Binding A   (*c*. 1898).
Cover: Black floral design with eastern lamp in centre.
Spine: Title, author (gold).
   Black ornamentation with winged horse on title page.
Address on Title Page: New York:/Manhattan Publishing Co.,/Publishers./

JORDAN MARSH COMPANY, Boston

A large department store which is said to have issued some Henty's.

THE MERSHON COMPANY, New York and Rahway, N.J.

The Mershon Company is one of the companies most inter-connected with others. Originally William L. Mershon owned a large printing works in Rahway, New Jersey. The Cassell Publishing Company, an American subsidiary of the British House Cassell & Co., went out of business in 1893 when its president absconded with $180,000. The principal creditor was William L. Mershon who reformed the company. In 1898 Cassell & Company reopened a New York branch and sued Mershon which led to the creation of The Mershon Company. Henty's only connection with Cassell was as a contributor to *Battles of the Nineteenth Century* and there is no record of either Cassell & Co., New York or The Cassell Publishing Company was using titles by him. As printers and binders Mershon did considerable work for other houses and one finds that the Stitt format B is a common Mershon binding although no Henty titles have been discovered in this form. It was as printers and binders that Mershon developed their links with other companies. After the failure of the Stitt Company, Mershon sold out completely to Chatterton and Peck in October 1906.

Binding A (*c*. 1898).
Cover: Black tendril design, containing three circles:
  Top: Head of European.
  Left: Head of Red Indian.
  Right: Head of Indian.
  Right and left red axe, sword and spear.
  Title (black on red shield).
  Horn under shield (black).
  Author (red).
Spine: Title, author (gold).
  Decoration of rapier and laurel wreath.
Address on Title Page: New York/The Mershon Company/Publishers/

Binding B (*c*. 1900).
Cover: Title (black).
  Author (red).
  Decoration of crossed sword and rifles.
  A shield with a device of a winged helmet over the inter-section.
  The whole of this decoration is surmounted by an eagle inside a laurel wreath, there is a sword on either side.
Spine: Title and author (gold).
  Decoration similar to cover.
Address on Title Page: New York/The Mershon Company/Publishers/

Binding C   (*c*. 1901).
Cover: Decoration of two boys, one standing aiming a rifle, the other kneeling in front of a tent holding his rifle, background, trees and three deer (grey and black).
All contained in grey frame.
Spine: Title (gold).
Author 'Henty' (gold).
Decoration of head and shoulders of boy in sweater and hat (outlined in black against grey background, framed in leaf and branch decoration).
Address on Title Page: New York/The Mershon Company/Publishers/

This binding as for the cover of *Malcom The Waterboy* by D. T. Henty, it almost certainly was not used for any of Mershon's 'Henty Series'. I include it here for purposes of comparison.

Binding D   (*c*. 1901).
Cover: Title, author (red).
Decoration of an oval panel showing an Indian, with a knife, threatening a red coated soldier.
Spine: Title, author (gold).
Publisher (red).
Decoration of two swords.
Address on Title Page: New York/The Mershon Company/Publishers/

Binding E   (*c*. 1902).
Cover: Red cloth.
Black line around cover.
Title, author, flower device (black).
Spine: Band at top and bottom (black).
Title, author, publisher (gold).
Address on Title Page: New York/The Mershon Company/Publishers/

Binding F   (*c*. 1902).
Cover: Title (black).
Decoration of repeated tulip design (black).
Spine: Author, title (gold).
Decoration as on cover.
Address on Title Page: New York/The Mershon Company/Publishers/

Binding G   (*c*. 1902).
Cover: Title (black).
Decoration of cavalry officer on black horse leading a charge.
Spine: Title, author (gold).
Publisher (black).

Decoration of two rifles, oar and anchor, linked together by a rope and laurel wreath.

Address on Title Page: New York/The Mershon Company/Publishers/

Binding H 1905
Cover: Title (black). Decoration of cavalry officer on black horse leading a charge.
Spine: Title, author, publisher 'The Mershon Co.' (black). Decoration of two rifles, oar and anchor, linked together by a rope and laurel wreath.
Address on Title Page: New York/Stitt Publishing Company/1905/

Binding I (*c*. 1907) 'The famous Henty Books, The Boy's Own Library'.
Cover: Title (black).
Decoration of cavalry officer on black horse leading a charge.
Spine: Title, author (gold).
Publisher (black).
Decoration of two rifles, oar and anchor, linked together by a rope and laurel wreath.
Address on Title Page: The Mershon Company/Rahway, N.J. New York./

I have been unable to discover when Mershon opened their Rahway office which would date this and the following format. The date is approximate and based on end paper inscriptions.

Binding J (*c*. 1907).
Cover: Title (black).
Two coloured decorations of a plant design based on the lotus shape.
Spine: Title, author (gold).
Publisher (black).
Decoration similar to cover.
Address on Title Page: The Mershon Company/Rahway, N.J. New York./

MUNRO SON'S

This company brought out a paperback Henty series.

MUTUAL BOOK COMPANY, Boston

NATIONAL BOOK COMPANY, New York

Copies of Henty's issued by the above three houses would seem to be scarce as I have no examples in my own collection. There is no evidence that they ever published by arrangement with Henty or his official publishers.

NEW AMSTERDAM BOOK COMPANY, New York

This company published the official American edition of *The Lost Heir*. This book is identical in every way with the James Bowden British first edition. Address on title Page: New Amsterdam Book Co.,/156 Fifth Avenue, New York./

NEW YORK PUBLISHING COMPANY, New York

Binding A (*c*. 1895).
   Cover: Red cloth-covered boards with design embossed on cover.
   Spine: Title, author, 'Empire Edition' (gold).
   Address on Title Page: New York/New York Publishing Company/26 City Hall Place/

This company may have been connected with The American News Company which was best known as a distributor. Some dime novels carry the imprint 'The American News Company/Publisher's Agent' instead of the actual publisher. They were active in the late 1880's early 1890's. Their Peoples' Edition often duplicated titles published in the N.Y. Book Company's Empire Edition (price 50c) and Library Edition (price $1). No copies of Henty in either The American News Company's Peoples' Edition or the N.Y. Publishing Company's Library Edition have been located. The New York Book Company went out of business in 1895, The American News Company acquiring the rights to the Empire and Library Editions.

J. S. OGILVIE PUBLISHING COMPANY, New York

Binding A (*c*. 1893).
   Cover: Black scroll work design.
      Centre: A black panel with 'Clarendon Edition' (cover colour).
   Spine: Design similar to cover, 'Clarendon Edition' (black). Title (gold).
   Address on Title Page: New York:/J. S. Ogilvie Publishing Company,/57 Rose Street./

OPTIMUS PRINTING COMPANY

The house published at least one title (*In the Days of the Mutiny*) in their paperback 'Paragon Library'.

PATTERSON AND WHITE, Philadelphia

Binding A 1897.
   Cover: Two men duelling, against a semi-circular background. Title (gold outlined in black).
      Author (gold).

Spine: Zulu shield shape panel with title (gold).
  Author, superimposed on crossed sabres (gold).
  Publisher (gold).
Address on Title Page: Philadelphia:/Paterson & White/
  1897/

PORTER & COATES

The only title traced to this house is *By Pike & Dyke*. This company was succeeded by Henry T. Coates of Philadelphia in 1895/96.

RAND, McNALLY AND COMPANY, Chicago and New York

This company are particularly associated with the American editions of *Dorothy's Double*. All the formats described below are used for different editions of this title.

Binding A   (*c*. 1895)
Cover: Red linen cloth-covered boards.
  Title, author, circle with interlaced vines (gold).
  All enclosed in gold frame.
Spine: Title, author, publisher, leaf decoration, (gold).
Address on Title Page: Chicago and New York/Rand,
  McNally & Company/

Binding B   'Alpha Library' (*c*. 1900).
Cover: Floral archway with flowers in centre (archway – light
  colour: flowers – white).
  Title (white).
Spine: Flower as cover.
  Title, author, publisher (white).
Address on Title Page: Chicago and New York:/Rand,
  McNally & Company/Publishers./

Binding C   'Alpha Library' (*c*. 1900)
Cover: Dark blue cloth-covered boards.
  Title, Fleur de Lis device, Author (white).
  Red frame round outside of cover.
Spine: Title, author (white, between two red bands). Publisher
  (white between two red bands).
Address on Title Page: Chicago and New York:/Rand,
  McNally & Company,/Publishers:/

Binding D   'The Antique Library' (*c*. 1901).
Cover: Panel (black and gold antique design).
  Title, author (gold).
Spine: Panel similar to cover.
  Title, author, publisher (gold).
Address on Title Page: Chicago and New York/Rand,
  McNally & Company/

This would seem to be the first illustrated edition.

ROBERTS BROTHERS, Boston

Published the same titles as Charles E. Brown, in the 1800's, possibly by arrangement with Henty or his publishers.

GEORGE ROUTLEDGE AND SONS LIMITED, New York, London and Manchester

One thinks of this house as a British firm. They published at least two items by Henty. *The Young Colonists* 1885 and 'For Name and Fame' as a serial in the 1885 *Every Boy's Annual*. At least two editions of *The Young Colonists* were printed in America, one (*c.* 1892) with an American title page address: George Routledge and Sons Limited/New York: 9 Lafayette Place/London and Manchester/

It would appear from the evidence of an 1899 Blackie Catalogue in an American Routledge impression, that Blackie continued to issue the American Routledge Edition after they had taken over the copyright of this title in 1896.

SCRIBNER & WELFORD
CHARLES SCRIBNER'S SONS
BLACKIE & SON LTD/CHARLES SCRIBNER'S SONS

These three publishing houses are usually taken together. The bulk of the official American Henty publications were published by one of these three.

SCRIBNER & WELFORD, New York. 1882–1890

Scribner & Welford, by arrangement with Blackie, imported the sheets and covers of all the Henty titles published by Blackie prior to the passage of the International Copyright Act of 1891. (For a complete list of these titles see below). The titles published under their imprint are identical with the Blackie editions apart from a tipped in title page and in most cases, the Scribner & Welford catalogue. A small percentage of these have been discovered in editions dated as per the English custom, with the New Year date rather than the actual date of publication. The Scribner & Welford firsts have yet to be properly classified and it is not impossible that more dated editions exist. Poor bibliography has led to much confusion about the American firsts prior to the passage of the copyright Act and there are still those under the impression that the Blackie/Scribner editions have first edition status. The undated Scribner & Welfords are difficult to identify as each title was reissued with a different catalogue but an identical title page each

Christmas. It is generally accepted by collectors that the later issues are not first editions and these can be identified by quotations from reviews of the book in the publisher's catalogue.

Cover and Spine: As Blackie.
Address on Title Page: New York/Scribner and Welford/743 & 745 Broadway./

BLACKIE/SCRIBNER, London and New York. (1891–1903)

Cover and Spine: As Blackie.
Address on Title Page: London: Blackie & Son, Limited;/New York: Charles Scribner's Sons,/153 to 157 Fifth Avenue./

The Blackie/Scribners are a reissue of the Scribner & Welfords. They are all undated.

CHARLES SCRIBNER'S SONS, New York

The Scribner & Welford Company had been set up to negotiate the American publication of English authors. George Welford negotiated the London side of the business while Charles Scribner handled the New York end. Charles Scribner died in 1871 and the business passed into the hands of his three sons. George Welford died in 1885 but the firm continued to use his name on the title page on books imported from England. The imminence of the copyright act resulted in Charles Scribner's Sons deciding to publish Henty for themselves in editions printed in America. They still continued to issue the earlier titles, imported, in association with Blackie (as described directly above). The first Scribner edition was an issue of three titles: *With Clive in India; One of the 28th;* and *In the Reign of Terror* all dated 1890. These were priced at $1.00 as opposed to the $1.50 of the Scribner & Welfords and the Blackie/Scribners.

Special Edition 1890
Cover and Spine: Similar to the U.K. firsts but cheaper and slightly less ornate.
Contents: The type is identical to the Blackie editions, but the paper inferior.
They are similar to the 1896–97 Canadian Editions.
Address on Title Page: New York/Charles Scribner's Sons/1890/

Popular Edition: 1894–1897 (?)
The evidence points to the fact that not all the Blackie/Scribner or Scribner & Welford titles were repeated in this edition. Priced at $1.00 its function seems to be the same as the special edition, to compete with the unofficial publication of the pre-copyright titles.

Only the most popular stories were included: *With Clive in India; By England's Aid; In Freedom's Cause; With Lee in Virginia; The Lion of St. Mark; One of the 28th; By Pike and Dyke; In the Reign of Terror; Under Drake's Flag; With Wolfe in Canada.* I have recorded various dates between 1894 and 1897 and there is every reason to presume that each title was repeated with no additions to the series. An interesting point that indicates a possible connection with the Worthington Company is that the sub-title on page (9) of *One of the 28th* is 'A Tale of Waterloo'.

Cover: Red cloth boards.
Decoration a frame of spears (silver and black), a banner suspended at the top between vertical spears (silver), with the title (lettered in black).
Below this a montage of weapons (silver and black), with a shield (silver) superimposed over the centre containing 'G. A. Henty' (black).
Beneath this a knapsack horn and drum (silver and black).
Spine: Panel (silver).
Title (black).
Montage of weapons with octagonal shield containing author (black on silver).
Publisher (silver).
Address on Title Page: New York/Charles Scribner's Sons/date/

Scribner Firsts 1891–1904

Printed in America by various printers e.g. J. S. Cushing & Co; The Caxton press and John Wilson and son. They are based on the Blackie designs with slight variations. Where Blackie often omit the publisher's name from the spine, Scribner always include it. Thus if Blackie have a spine designed: Title/decoration/'by/G. A. Henty', Scribner might alter this to Title/G. A. Henty/Design/publisher or if Blackie has Title/By/G. A. Henty/design, Scribner might alter this to Title/G. A. Henty/reduced decoration/publisher.

Address on title page: New York/Charles Scribner's Sons/date/

Scribner Cheap Edition 1902–

This edition like the special edition and the popular edition seems to be an attempt to combat the unofficial U.S. printings. All titles were eventually published in this uniform format.

Cover: Red cloth covered boards.
On either side of the cover two vertical swords (black), these are linked by an oak leaf chaplet (light green).
Superimposed on this, four shields bearing heads of a man in a

Tudor Hat,
a Medieval Hat,
a Norman Helmet and
a Military Topée.
Joining the swords, at the points a scroll (light green outlined in black with 'G. A. Henty' lettered in black).
Beneath this 'copyright 1902 by Charles Scribner's Sons' (black).
In the centre of the chaplet, title (black).
Spine: Title (gold).
Author (black).
Sword (outlined in Black) with oak leaf chaplet around hilt (light green).
Publisher (black).
Address on Title Page: New York/Charles Scribner's Sons/date/

This edition would seem identical in contents with the Grosset and Dunlap edition described above.

The Scribner Series For Young People 1919–

At least five Henty titles were published in this series: *With Lee in Virginia; With Wolfe in Canada; Redskin and Cowboy* and *Under Drake's Flag*. Although not listed in any of the advertisements of copies examined, I also possess a copy of *By Pike and Dyke* dated 1923 published in this series. The original illustrations were reproduced in colour.
Cover: Red cloth-covered boards.
A pictorial card of the coloured frontpiece with author and title superimposed in gold.
Spine: Title, author, publisher (gold).
Address on Title Page: New York/Charles Scribner's Sons/date/

A cheaper reissue of this series (c. 1930)
Cover: Red cloth-covered boards.
Title, author (blue).
Spine: Title, author, publisher (blue).
Address on Title Page: New York/Charles Scribner's Sons/

Scribners although not the first American publisher to produce Henty titles were certainly the principle firm to officially handle his work. In most cases the Scribner edition was published some weeks before their Blackie counterpart. This makes them the true first edition. Possibly because they are easier to obtain, the British editions tend to be preferred by collectors but the Scribner firsts are now coming into their own.

STITT PUBLISHING COMPANY, New York

It was founded in 1905 by W. M. Stitt, Joseph Scanell and W. L. Mershon. Stitt had originally been employed by Mershon. It seems possible that the elderly Mershon was beginning to dispose of his empire, however Stitt returned to his role as a senior salesman and the company was wound up in 1906.

Binding A   (1905).
Cover: Two faces in a circle on wampum belt.
Spine: Title, author, publisher (dark blue).
   Decoration: A piece of wampum.
Address on Title Page: New York/Stitt Publishing Co./1905/

Binding B   (1905).
Cover: Youth, dressed for hunting holding rifle (black), behind him is a laurel wreath containing a circular red panel. He is surrounded by sports equipment and standing on a pedestal on which is printed the title.
Spine: Ice hockey stick, gun and baseball bat (black), superimposed on football (red).
   Title, author, publisher (black).
Address on Title Page: New York/Stitt Publishing Company/1905/

Binding C   (1905).
Cover: Title (black).
   Decoration of Cavalry officer on black horse leading a charge.
Spine: Title, author, publisher 'The Mershon Co' (black).
   Decoration of two rifles, oar and anchor, linked together by a rope a laurel wreath.
Address on Title Page: New York/Stitt Publishing Company/1905/

STREET AND SMITH, New York and London

Binding A   Medal Library 1899.
Cover: Off-white paper wrappers.
   'Medal Library No. . . .'
   10 cents.
   Publisher (black).
   Decoration based on an illustration from the original edition in black and pink with title and author superimposed.
Spine: 'Medal Library No. . . .'
   Title, author (black).
Rear Cover: Publisher's advertisement.
Address on Title Page: New York/Street & Smith, publishers/238 William Street/

Binding B   Medal Library (1902).
Cover: Green paper wrappers.
   'Medal Library No. . . .', publisher (yellow).

Decoration a coloured picture to illustrate the text with title and author superimposed.

Spine: Off white.

'Medal Library No. . . .', title, author (blue).

Rear Cover: White with publisher's advertisement printed in blue.

Address on Title Page: New York/Street & Smith, publishers/238 William Street/

Binding C   (*c.* 1903).

Cover: Title, author (black).

Panel above title: Lakeside scene with two boats.

Panel below title: Pictorial card depicts white men lying firing at charging natives.

Spine: Title (gold).

Publisher (black).

Decoration of skis and snowshoes above tree lined lake with two yachts.

Address on Title Page: New York and London/Street and Smith, Publishers/

Binding D   (*c.* 1903). I have no means of dating this second format other than by the address on the title page which is identical with binding C.

Cover: Two panels: Top: A boy in a green double breasted suit, sitting on a bentwood chair reading a book (red).

Bottom: Title, author (red).

Spine: Title, author, publisher (red).

Address on Title Page: New York and London/Street and Smith, Publishers/

This house was best known for its paperback series 'The Medal Library'. These were first published in approximately 1889.

THE SUPERIOR PRINTING COMPANY, Akron and New York

Binding A   (before 1905).

Front & Rear Covers: Cream paper covered wrappers.

Coloured panel showing a young cowboy dressed in khaki riding a brown horse. He is waving his hat with his upraised right arm.

Title, author (blue) beneath panel.

Spine: 'Henty Series Number?', Title, author (blue).

Address on Title Page: The Superior Printing Co./Akron, O. New York, N.Y./

J. A. TAYLOR AND COMPANY, New York

This company published *A Hidden Foe* and *In the Days of the Mutiny* in the early '90's. It has not been established that they were ever involved in producing pirate editions of the boys' books. The publication of the adult titles could have been by arrangement.

THOMPSON AND THOMAS, Chicago

An edition of *The Young Buglers* published by this house has been reported. Charles C. Thompson was originally a bookseller, the firm appears to have been formed in 1901, possibly succeeding a firm Thompson & Hood. It became Charles C. Thompson Company in 1909.

UNION SCHOOL LIBRARY, Chicago

Cover: red cloth with calf spine.
Spine: Title, author, 'Union School Library' (gold).
Address on Title Page: Chicago/Union School Furnishing Co./Publishers/

UNITED STATES BOOK COMPANY, New York

This was an attempt by John Lovell (see above). Among the companies involved were his own, that of his brother and such familiar names as Allison, Donohue, Hurst, International, Munro, The National Book Company and Worthington. The combination was terminated in 1903.

JOHN WANAMAKER, Philadelphia, New York, Paris

I have three formats for this house. The first for the 'Columbine Library', has a fly leaf inscription 1904, but I consider it to have been issued nearer to its Alpha Library counterpart. The only title I have in this format is *Dorothy's Double*, which would seem to indicate that this was an adult series. A further complication with this particular book is that the 2 pp. catalogue is for the Rand-McNally 'New Alpha Library of 12 issues'. This catalogue is part of the final gathering of the book. I date 'the Young People's Library' later, because Paris is added in the title page address which would seem to indicate later publication, although this is inserted 1900.

Binding A   (*c*. 1900). 'Columbine Library'
Cover: Dark red cloth, covered boards. Embossed overlapping semi-circles with flower design.
Spine: Decoration as cover. Title, author, publisher (gold).
Address in Title Page: John Wanamaker,/Philadelphia. New York./

Binding B   (*c*. 1900). 'Wanamaker Young People's Library'.
Cover: Author, title (black).

Decoration of head and shoulders of boy and girl contained in black design.

Spine: Author, title, publisher (gold). Black design.

Address on Title Page: John Wanamaker/Philadelphia New York Paris/

Binding C   (*c*. 1900). 'The Wanamaker Young People's History'

Cover: Tan cloth covered board. Triangular scroll work design, containing a centre plaque 'The Wanamaker Young People's Library' on the heading a boy and girl (black and grey) - all contained in red frame.

Spine: Decoration similar to cover.
  Title, author, publisher (gold).
  Red bands top and bottom.

Address on title page: John Wanamaker/Philadelphia New York Paris/

A. WESSELS AND COMPANY, New York

This company published *Famous Battles of the Nineteenth Century* which was based on Cassell's *Battle of the Nineteenth Century* in 1904.

Cover: A soldier threatened by a bare-chested man.
  Title, volume number (cream).

Spine: Crossed swords superimposed over a lance.
  Title (gold).
  Publisher (black).

Address on Title Page: New York/A. Wessels Company/date/

THE WESTBROOK PUBLISHING COMPANY, Cleveland

An edition of *With Lee in Virginia* is reported as having been published by this house. *With Lee in Virginia* is highly sought after in America to this day, always appearing on American lists at a slightly higher price than other titles. It is possible that because of its American interest it was handled by publishers who otherwise ignored Henty.

WILLIAMS

A company presumably connected with Worthington Co. The only example in my possession has an inscription on p. 19 'June 11th 1897', but it would appear to be much earlier and contemporary with the 1890 Worthington Co. Editions.

Binding A   (*c*. 1890). *With Clive in India*
Cover: Red cloth-covered boards.
  Title and author (gold).

Decoration (black and grey) based on the Gordon Browne
frontispiece for *With Wolfe in Canada*.
Spine: Title (cover colour on gold block).
Author (gold).
Publisher (Williams – cover colour on gold band). Decoration
band on the figure (gold) on the spine of the Blackie first
edition.
Address on Title Page: New York/Worthington Company/747
Broadway/

One might interpret the discovery of this hybrid copy as an indication that Williams came into the publishing business in the same
way as Mershon and Donohue i.e. via bookbinding and printing,
but it should be noted that the verso of the title page credits
'Barr-Dinwiddie/Printing and Book-Binding Co.,/Jersey City,
N.J.'

JOHN C. WINSTON & COMPANY, Philadelphia

This company was connected with Henry T. Coates and Patterson
and White (see above).

WORTHINGTON COMPANY (WORTHINGTON AND COMPANY), New York

One of the most interesting of all Henty's American publishers.
There is a possibility that the publications from this house were by
arrangement with Blackie & Sons.

Binding A   (1890). *A Tale of Waterloo*
Cover: Blue-Green or tan cloth-covered boards.
Three panels:
Top panel: Scroll design (black), superimposed on this panel a
flag (red outlined in black) with title (cover colour), a red
band, then
Second panel: (black), with leaf design (cover colour),
superimposed on this a Greek coin (red) with the helmeted
head of Mars (cover colour outlined in black), 'Mars' (cover
colour outlined in black), a red band, a row of dots (black),
then
Bottom panel: (cover colour), author (red).
Spine: Panels similar to cover.
Top panel has title and author (cover colour on gold). Second
panel, coin with head of Hermes, 'illustrated' (cover colour on
gold).
Bottom panel as cover with publisher (gold).
Address on Title Page: New York/Worthington Company/747
Broadway/

Binding B   (1890). *By England's Aid*
Cover: Blue-green or tan cloth-covered boards.
  Three panels:
  Top panel: Scroll design (black), superimposed on this panel a flag (red outlined in black) with title (cover colour), a red band, then
  Second panel: (black), with leaf design (cover colour), superimposed on this a Greek coin (red) with the helmeted head of Mars (cover colour outlined in black), 'Mars' (cover colour outlined in black), a red band, a row of dots (black), then
  Bottom panel: (cover colour), author (red).
Spine: Panels similar to cover.
  Top panel has title and author (cover colour on gold).
  Second panel, coin with head of Hermes, 'illustrated' (cover colour on gold).
  Bottom panel as cover with publisher (gold).
Address on Title Page: New York/Worthington Company, 747 Broadway/1890/

Some copies have 'Barr-Dinwiddie Printing & Book-Binding Co.,/Greenville, Jersey City, N.J.' underneath the note on the verso of the title page.

Binding C   (1890). *The Lion of St. Mark*
Cover: Blue-green or tan cloth-covered boards.
  Three panels:
  Top panel: Scroll design (black), superimposed on this panel a flag (red outlined in black) with title (cover colour), a red band, then
  Second panel: (black), with leaf design (cover colour), superimposed on this a Greek coin (red) with the helmeted head of Mars (cover colour outlined in black), 'Mars' (cover colour outlined in black), a red band, a row of dots (black), then
  Bottom panel: (cover colour), author (red).
Spine: Panels similar to cover.
  Top panel has title and author (cover colour on gold).
  Second panel, coin with head of Hermes, 'illustrated' (cover colour on gold).
  Bottom panel as cover with publisher (gold).
Address on Title Page: New York,/Worthington Co., 747 Broadway,/1890./

Binding D   (1890). *In the Reign of Terror*
Cover: Blue-green or tan cloth-covered boards.

Three panels:
Top panel: Scroll design (black), superimposed on this panel a flag (red outlined in black) with title (cover colour), a red band, then
Second panel: (black), with leaf design (cover colour), superimposed on this a Greek coin (red) with the helmeted head of Mars (cover colour outlined in black), 'Mars' (cover colour outlined in black), a red band, a row of dots (black) then
Bottom panel: (cover colour), author (red).
Spine: Panels similar to cover.
Top panel has title and author (cover colour on gold).
Second panel, coin with head of Hermes, 'Illustrated' (cover colour on gold).
Bottom panel as cover with publisher (gold).
Address on Title Page: New York/Worthington & Company/747 Broadway/1890/

Binding E   (before 1890). *By Pike and Dyke*

My copies are both inscribed '1894'. The title page address is identical. My feeling is that they are probably earlier. The title page address for this company varies with each title inspected but the address of this title is the closest to the undated *A Tale of Waterloo* one copy of which is inscribed 'Xmas 1900'. It is possible that *A Tale of Waterloo (One of the 28th)* and this edition of *By Pike and Dyke* are both first American publications 1889. This edition has a curious 'note' pasted on to page iv:

NOTE. – 'By Pike and Dyke' is based on John Lothrop Motley's 'Rise of the Dutch,' and readers who desire to gain a more intimate acquaintance with the heroic William of Orange and the inspiring story of his career should turn to that monumental work in the history of American letters. Motley himself shared the enthusiastic admiration which a study of the life of William of Orange always excites in the hearts of true Americans. In one of the letters preserved in 'Motley's Correspondence' he says of him, 'He is one of the very few men who have a right to be mentioned in the same page with Washington' 'no one has done more to establish that right in the mind of the world at large than the distinguished author of 'The Rise of the Dutch Republic'.

A similar, but less jingoistically American note is printed on the verso of the title page of *By England's Aid* 1890. That the note is an afterthought, almost an extra slip to *By Pike and Dyke* rather than an actual part of the book could indicate publication before 1890. It being decided to incorporate a similar addition to the preface as part of *By England's Aid*.

Cover:　Red cloth-covered boards.
　Top: Black Line or design with branch centre.
　Foot: Floral frieze (black).
Spine:　Title, author, publisher (gold).
Address on Title Page: Blackie publisher's device/New York/Worthington Co/747 Broadway./

Binding F (c. 1890). *With Clive in India*
Cover:　Red cloth-covered boards.
　Title and author (gold).
　Decoration (black and grey) based on the Gordon Browne frontispiece for *With Wolfe in Canada.*
Spine:　Title (cover colour on gold block).
　Author (gold).
　Publisher (Williams – cover colour on gold board).
　Decoration based on the figure (gold) on the spine of the Blackie first edition.
Address on Title Page:　New York/Worthington Company/747 Broadway/

Binding G (c. 1895).
Cover:　Brown cloth embossed in black as follows: three different horizontal frieze designs occupy the top third of the cover; the same designs are repeated in reverse order in the bottom; the centre is occupied by a still different horizontal design with a circle in the centre.
Spine:　Top: black embossed design/horizontal black line/title and author in gold/horizontal black line/another black design/Donohue/Henneberry/& Co./in black/another design in black at bottom.
Address on Title Page:　New York/Worthington Company/747 Broadway/or New York,/Worthington Co., 747 Broadway,/1890,/or New York/Worthington Company, 747 Broadway/1890/
End Papers:　Yellow and cream pebble design.

This would appear to be a late remainder issue from the Worthington plates. Note that although the title pages refer to illustrations, there are no illustrations used.

This ends the catalogue of known U.S. Henty formats.

An obvious fact, which previous Henty bibliographers have failed to note, is that very few Henty titles published after 1890 are included in the numerous pirate Henty series. The titles that are included, either have no British counterpart, or are differenced in some way from the U.K. edition, or are adult novels published under copyright or, in the case of the Grosset & Dunlap Henty's, are produced by arrangement with Scribners.

A Henty series would include:

Out on the Pampas (first published in England by Griffith & Farran, 1871. Probably not published in America till 1882 by E. P. Dutton & Co.)

The Young Franc-Tireurs (first published in England by Griffith & Farran, 1872. Also first issued in America in 1882 by E. P. Dutton & Co.)

The Young Buglers (first published in England by Griffith & Farran, 1880(1879). First issued in America in the same edition by E. P. Dutton & Co., 1879. This is perhaps the first Henty title to be issued in America)

The Cornet of Horse (issued simultaneously by Sampson Low, Marston, Searle and Rivington, London and J. B. Lippincott and Company in 1881. Although *The Young Buglers* was issued with the names of both Griffith & Farran and E. P. Dutton & Co. on the title page, this would seem to be the first Henty to be published in America with only the American publisher's name on the title page)

In Times of Peril (first published in England by Griffith & Farran, 1881. First issued in America in the same edition 1881 by E. P. Dutton & Co.)

Facing Death (Blackie 1882 and Scribner & Welford (1882))

Under Drake's Flag (Blackie 1883(1882) and Scribner & Welford (1882)

The Boy Knight (first published in England under the title *Winning His Spurs* by Sampson Low, Marston, Searle & Rivington, 1882. First published in America by Roberts Bros. 1882. Also issued in 1892 by Charles E. Brown in 'The Roundabout Books' under the title *Fighting the Saracens)*

Friends Though Divided (first published in England by Griffith & Farran, 1883. First issued in America by E. P. Dutton & Co., in the same edition 1883)

Jack Archer (first published in England by Sampson Low, Marston, Searle & Rivington, 1883. First traced publication of this title in America by Roberts Bros., 1884. It seems more than likely that there is an 1883 edition either by Roberts Bros. or Lippincott as this would be consistent with the pattern established for the other Sampson Low Henty's. Also published by Roberts Bros. under the title *The Fall of Sebastopol 1884)*

With Clive in India (Blackie 1884(1883) and Scribner & Welford (1883))

By Sheer Pluck (Blackie 1885(1884) and Scribner & Welford (1884))

In Freedom's Cause (Blackie 1885(1884) and Scribner & Welford (1884))

True to the Old Flag (Blackie 1885(1884) and Scribner & Welford (1884))

St George for England (Blackie 1885(1884) and Scribner & Welford (1884))

The Young Colonists (first published in 1885 by George Routledge who had offices in both London and New York, later American editions are printed at The Caxton Press/171, 173 Macdougal Street, New York (*c.*1892) and Burr Printing House,/New York, U.S.A. (*c.* 1899) both these editions being published by Routledge, it is possible that a variant first edition of this title, printed in America exists)

The Dragon and the Raven (Blackie 1886(1885) and Scribner & Welford (1885))

For Name and Fame (Blackie 1886(1885) and Scribner & Welford (1885))

The Lion of the North (Blackie 1886(1885) and Scribner & Welford (1885))

Through the Fray (Blackie 1886(1885) and Scribner & Welford (1885))

Yarns on the Beach (Blackie 1886(1885) and Scribner & Welford (1885))

With Wolfe in Canada (Blackie 1887(1886) and Scribner & Welford 1887(1886))

The Bravest of the Brave (Blackie 1887(1886) and Scribner & Welford (1886))

A Final Reckoning (Blackie 1887(1886) and Scribner & Welford (1886))

The Young Carthaginian (Blackie 1887(1886) and Scribner & Welford 1887(1886))

Bonnie Prince Charlie (Blackie 1888(1887) and Scribner & Welford (1887))

Orange & Green (Blackie 1888(1887) and Scribner & Welford (1887))

In the Reign of Terror (Blackie 1888(1887) and Scribner & Welford (1887). Also published by H. M. Caldwell under the title *The Reign of Terror)*

Sturdy and Strong (Blackie 1888(1887) and Scribner & Welford (1887))

For the Temple (Blackie 1888(1887) and Scribner & Welford (1887))

The Lion of St. Mark (Blackie 1889(1888) and Scribner & Welford (1888))

Captain Bayley's Heir (Blackie 1889(1888) and Scribner & Welford 1889(1888))

The Cat of Bubastes (Blackie 1889(1888) and Scribner & Welford 1889(1888))

Tales of Danger and Daring (Blackie 1889 and Scribner & Welford (1889))

By Pike and Dyke (Blackie 1890(1889) and Scribner & Welford (1889)). Also published by Worthington N.D.

One of the 28th (Blackie 1890(1889) and Scribner & Welford (1889). Also published by Charles Scribner's Sons 1890 in an edition which is sometimes erroneously taken to be the American first and by Worthington Company under the title *A Tale of Waterloo (1890)*)

With Lee in Virginia (Blackie 1890(1889) and Scribner & Welford (1889))

By England's Aid (Blackie 1891(1890) and Scribner & Welford (1890). Also published by Worthington Company 1890)

The Young Midshipman (first published in England under the title *A Chapter of Adventures* (Blackie 1891(1890) and in America by Scribner & Welford (1890). The earliest edition of this title, located to date, is from the mid-1890s. There are two possibilities, the most likely is that the first edition *c.* 1891 and probably by one of the earlier Henty pirate publishers, such as Worthington, International or Roberts Bros. has yet to be located. An alternative explanation is that this title was not pirated at the time of its first issue, but as it had been published prior to the International Copyright Act of 1891 it was not protected by this Act. The publisher who first decided to issue it in an unauthorised format deciding to alter the title so as not to call too much attention to this final act of piracy)

Maori and Settler (Blackie 1891(1890) and Scribner & Welford (1890))

By Right of Conquest (Blackie 1891(1890) and Scribner & Welford (1890))

The above Henty's are those published before the International Copyright Act and therefore not protected by it. They comprise the bulk of every cheap American Henty series. One other title, unprotected by the Act but not generally included in the cheap Henty series (apart from the various Hurst series) was *The Curse of Carne's Hold* (first published in Britain by Spencer, Blackett & Hallam, 2 vols., 1889 and in America by John W. Lovell (1889)). There is nothing particularly exceptional about unofficial U.S. issues of the above titles. Seemingly unofficial editions of later

Henty titles from American publishing houses have a much greater significance.

In the Days of the Mutiny, The Brahmin's Treasure, Rujub the Juggler, Colonel Thorndyke's Secret (Captain Thorndyke's Secret), Dorothy's Double, Two Sieges of Paris, A Girl of the Commune and *The Lost Heir* must have been produced either with the authority of Henty or of his official publishers and there is no reason to suspect any sharp practice in their re-publication. Because it cost money to reproduce these titles they were not automatically included in every Henty series, hence their comparative scarcity even in American editions.

We are left with four American collections of short stories *Among Malay Pirates* (also published under the title *Among the Malays*), at first sight this would appear to be another pirate edition, but all the stories except the title story had already appeared prior to the Act in *Tales of Danger & Daring* and permission would only be needed for the title story. *The Golden Cannon*, first published by Mershon, under copyright, with two non-Henty stories also draws on *Tales of Danger & Daring* for 'White Faced Dick' and 'A Brush with the Chinese': *Redskins & Colonists* published after Henty's death is published under copyright. In its unofficial Henty series variant *Sturdy & Strong* includes 'Do Your Duty' 'A Fish Wife's Dream' and 'Surly Joe' from *Yarns on the Beach*.

Yarns on the Beach and *Tales of Danger and Daring* are not pirated under these titles but their stories appear in the above collections and as fillers in other titles (e.g. 'A Fish Wife's Dream' in *The Lost Heir*).

Among the most interesting American editions of Henty are the Grosset & Dunlap editions of *By Conduct and Courage, The Treasure of the Incas,* and *Redskin and Cowboy* and the John Wanamaker edition of *By Conduct and Courage*. These are in fact variant Scribner editions and issued by arrangement with that company.

Section II

Chapter i

Bevis by Richard Jefferies.

Edited by G. A. Henty.

Richard Jefferies, the author of *Bevis*, like the hero of his book, had little formal education. Indeed *Bevis* is an idealised version of his own boyhood roaming the countryside and reading everything he could lay his hands on.

He was a lonely boy disliking cricket and all the accepted boyish pastimes. He was an unsuccessful novelist, trying to write about a society of which he knew nothing. His first breakthrough came when he wrote a long letter to *The Times* in November 1872. This dealt with the problems of the agricultural labourers of Wiltshire. After this Jefferies became recognised as an authority on country matters. For the last six or seven years of his life he was sick and relatively poor. He died at the early age of thirty-eight.

What possible connection could there be between the (in terms of his own age) unsociable Jefferies and George Henty, except, possibly the dislike of cricket? Yet there is strong evidence that Henty was responsible for editing *Bevis* for Sampson Low, Marston. *Bibliography of G. A. Henty and Hentyana* by R. S. Kennedy and B. J. Farmer contains the following entry:

BEVIS: 1888
This edition of Bevis by Richard Jefferies, is said to be edited by

Henty. We have never seen the book; nor is there any record of it in the British Museum. Jefferies died in 1887. It seems at least doubtful if Henty would feel qualified to edit the work of the great naturalist. In the 1891 edition of Bevis, Messrs Sampson Low, the publishers, make no mention of Henty.

S. J. Looker in his study of Jefferies' England has a check list at the end. He makes no reference to Henty as an editor of Bevis, though he gives the 1904 edition of Bevis published by Duckworth, with an introduction by E. V. Lucas. H. S. Salt, in his *Richard Jefferies, A Study,* makes no reference to Henty.

G. A. Henty. A Bibliography compiled by Robert L. Dartt states:
BEVIS
Whether Henty did or did not edit a boy's book titled *Bevis* by Richard Jefferies, remains to be answered. Farmer gave 1888 as the edition, but there are no copies of that date in the British Museum, nor did the editions inspected by the writer carry any notation concerning Henty.
However in the (A.C.) of *Winning His Spurs,* dated 1897, published by Sampson Low, an entry in the 32-page catalogue at the end of text reads 'Bevis, by Richard Jefferies, Edited by G. A. Henty'. And Mr Frank Vernon Lay, London, has shown the writer a small advertising insert issued by Sampson Low, which notes 'No. 54 Bevis, by the late Richard Jefferies. Edited by G. A. Henty. 'The book is full of the comment of the author's peculiar charm. *Daily News.'*

Sampson Low do not always attach catalogues to their publications. A check through one hundred of their publications between 1888 the date suggested by Farmer and 1904 the date of the Duckworth edition supplied the following additional references to an edition of *Bevis* edited by Henty:

The Cornet of Horse by G. A. Henty N.D. (*c.* 1895)
'Uniform with this volume'
Bevis by Richard Jefferies. Edited by G. A. Henty.
Winning His Spurs by G. A. Henty 1888.

No catalogue reference to *Bevis.* Another book by Jefferies *Amaryllis at the Fair* is advertised.

Winning His Spurs 1893
'Uniform with this volume'
Bevis by Richard Jefferies. Edited by G. A. Henty.
Winning His Spurs 1896
'Uniform with this volume'
Bevis by Richard Jefferies. Edited by G. A. Henty.
Winning His Spurs 1897
 Uniform with this volume'
Bevis by Richard Jefferies. Edited by G. A. Henty.

Jack Archer 1888 and 1889
No reference to *Bevis* or Jefferies in either edition.
Jack Archer 1892
'Uniform with this volume'
Bevis by Richard Jefferies. Edited by G. A. Henty.
Jack Archer 1894
'Uniform with this volume'
Bevis by Richard Jefferies. Edited by G. A. Henty.
Jack Archer N.D. (inscribed 1896)
'Uniform with this volume'
Bevis by the late Richard Jefferies.

These references seem to be a simple statement of fact rather than an attempt to sell the book on Henty's reputation. Henty had done a certain amount of work for Sampson Low, editing *The Union Jack* in the early 1880s, as well as publishing the three books mentioned above and being one of the leading contributors to their magazine *Boys* (1892–94). Many good judges considered *Bevis* too long for boys, e.g. 'This is the best boy's book in the world, but it's a bit too long, and if I were you I should skip' recommended Sir Walter Besant to a young Guy Pocock. It was quite natural for Sampson and Low to ask their leading boy's author to edit it.

In the introduction to the 1904 edition, published by Duckworth and Company, E. V. Lucas states:

> ... Written in the old three-decker days, it was published in 1882 in three volumes, thus obeying a convention to which we now look back with astonishment and effectively preventing its true reader – the boy – from approaching it. A few years later it was re-issued in a more reasonable form, in one volume, with pictures; but the book had ceased to be as Jefferies wrote it, abridgment having been made without the reader's knowledge – that unpardonable fault. 'Bevis', which has been seen through the press by the author's only son, Mr Harold Jefferies, now makes its third appeal.

E. V. Lucas states very clearly that the Duckworth and Company edition is the third edition and that the one volume edition carries no indication that it is abridged. This would seem to indicate that the Sampson Low edition never did carry Henty's name on the title page. The copy examined below simply states 'New and Cheaper Edition'.
If this is Henty's *Bevis* then we must look for the evidence internally, external evidence having established the existence of an edition edited by him. It is inconceivable that a reputable publisher, like Sampson Low, would have advertised a book for five years if it had never existed. Once might mean that the edition had been

planned but never completed, the appearance of advertisements between 1893 and 1898 would rule out this possibility. Yet Lucas states that the abridgement was made without the readers knowledge, and seems unaware that Henty was associated with the one volume edition.

A comparison between the Duckworth and Company edition, which restored the text of the 1882 three volume edition, and the Sampson Low, Marston and Company one volume edition shows considerable textual variation.

Chapter I 'Bevis at Work'

In the Jefferies version, towards the end of this chapter when he has finished making the raft from the packing case he decides to 'go indoors and sit down and play at something else'. There then follows a description of the kitchen and the parlour. In the parlour the bookcase had been left open, he takes out an old book of historical romance.

> Bevis put himself so into it, that he did it all, *he* bribed the porter, *he* played the harp, and drew the sword; these were no words to him, it was a living picture in which he himself acted.

This whole rather poetical section is cut in the Sampson Low Marston version to:

> . . . and thought he would go indoors and read for a while as a change.
>
> He stayed there but a short hour, and his mind, so soon as he had put down the book, ran still on his raft, and out he raced to see it again, fresh and bright from the rest of leaving it alone a little while.

Chapter II   'The Launch'

Apart from two paragraphs being combined into one there seems no variation in this chapter.

Chapter III   'The Mississippi'

When Mark and Bevis are digging through roots to free the raft Bevis decides that they are Greeks digging a canal through Mount Athos. He is Alexander the Great and Mark is Pisistratus. This game of make believe is removed in the Sampson Low, Marston edition.

Chapter IV   'Discovery of the New Sea'

The next day when Mark and Bevis prepare to continue their explorations. They discuss the preparation of a medicine chest. Again this make believe element is removed from the Sampson

Low edition. Towards the end of this chapter they begin their explorations which are continued in the next chapters.

Chapter V 'By the New Nile'
Chapter VI 'Central Africa'
Chapter VII 'The Jungle'
Chapter VIII 'The Witch'

These chapters with their beautiful descriptions of the countryside intermingled with the boy's make believe are not present in the Sampson Low version.

Chapter IX 'Swimming'

This chapter which describes the boys learning to swim is summarised in:

> He (Bevis's father) therefore took them in hand going down with them every day to the water, until both could swim fairly.

and included at the beginning of the next chapter.

Chapter X (Chapter V Sampson Low)   'Savages'

Before the boys start their game of 'Savages' they discuss alternatives such as: 'Lions and Tigers', 'Shipwrecked people on an island', 'escaping prisoners' and 'hermits'; this discussion is omitted in the Sampson Low version, as is the invention of a language for the 'Savages':

> 'Kalabala-blong!' said Mark
> 'Hududu-blow-fluz!' replied Bevis ....
> ....
> 'Umplumum!' he shouted coming up again.
> 'Ikiklikah,' and Mark disappeared.
> 'Noklikah,' said Bevis..

It should perhaps be noted that useful arts such as how to make flint sling darts are retained in full.

Chapter XI (Chapter VI Sampson Low)   'Savages continued – The Catamaran' The discussion of the landing on a savage shore which starts:

> 'We ought to see ourselves on the shore with spears and things when we are sailing round,' said Mark.

and ranges over such topics as making poison for arrows and spears, a battlefield with broken lances and riderless horses, flocks of crows and heaps of white bones, Genii and magic is omitted from the Sampson Low edition. The courting game which the boys watch from behind the hedge when looking for nightshade is also omitted.

Chapter XII (*VII* Sampson Low)   'Savages continued – Making the Sails'

The dialogue between Mark, Bevis and their two friends is halved in Sampson Low. The beating of the Donkey by Bevis and Mark is cut as is Mark's terror at not finding Bevis when he returns to the bathing-place. The rather savage dialogue after the boys have killed the moor-cock is also removed from the Sampson Low text. This well observed description of children's cruelty typifies Jefferies's genius to catch all facets of boyhood including the extremes of poetry and barbarism, the cutting tends to place the work in the centre of these two extremes.

Chapter XIII (*VIII* Sampson Low)   'Savages continued – The Mast Fitted'

The dialogue between Mark and Bevis, after they have lit the fire omits the references to 'fetich', and is slightly condensed.

Chapter XIV (*IX* Sampson Low)   'The Council of War'

The dialogue with which Jefferies opens this chapter is cut

Chapter XV (*X* Sampson Low)   'The War Begins'

The period before tea, when Bevis, left on his own, reads the Odyssey is omitted.

Chapter XVI (*XI* Sampson Low)   'The Battle of Pharsalia'

No difference between the texts except that the Sampson Low edition has slightly more paragraphs. This slight simplification is present throughout the edition.

Chapter XVII (*XII* Sampson Low)   'The Battle continued – Scipio's Charge'

No significant differences between the two texts.

Chapter XVIII (*XIII* Sampson Low)   'The Battle continued – Mark Antony'

No significant differences between the two texts.

Chapter XIX (*XIV* Sampson Low) 'Bevis in the Storm'

No significant differences between the two texts.

Chapter XX   (*XV Sampson Low*)   'Mark is put in Prison'

No significant differences between the two texts.

Chapter XXI (*XVI* Sampson Low) 'In Disgrace – Visit to Jack's'

Oddly enough the pattern of paragraph variation is reversed, the Sampson Low paragraphs being longer in this chapter. The reason would seem to be that the paragraphs are descriptive. The paragraph division, noted above, tends to be made when there is speech in mid-paragraph. Apart from this there is no difference between the two versions.

Chapter XXII (*XVII Sampson Low*) 'Sailing'

The dialogue at the end of the chapter is slightly shortened to omit Mark and Bevis's imaginary lifeboat smash with the people being 'Pounded into jelly-fish'.

Chapter XXIII (*XVIII* Sampson Low) 'Sailing continued – "There She Lay, all the Day!" '

No significant difference between the two texts.

Chapter XXIV (*XIX* Sampson Low) 'Sailing continued – Voyage to the Unknown Island'

The imaginative conversation at the beginning of the voyage, which ranges over such diverse topics as Malay Pirates, sandalwood, diamonds, unknown sea creatures and a magician is cut from the Sampson Low text, as is the talk of sharks, tigers, boaconstrictors 'and heaps of jolly things' when Mark comes back from going round the island. The end of this dialogue is also heavily pruned, in particular the section about Frances:

'I'll try,' said Bevis. 'How ought you to get a girl to do anything?'
'Stare at her,' said Mark. 'That's what Jack does, like a donk at a thistle when he can't eat any more.'
'Does Frances like the staring?'
'She pretends she doesn't, but she does. You stare at her and act stupid'.
'Is Jack stupid?'
'When he's at our house,' said Mark. 'He's as stupid as an owl. Now she kisses you, and you just whisper and squeeze her hand, and say it's very tiny. You don't know how conceited she is about her hand – can't you see – she's always got it somewhere where you can see it; and she sticks her foot out so' (Mark put one foot out); 'and don't you move an inch, but stick close to her, and get her into a corner or in the arbour. Mind, though, if you don't keep on telling her how pretty she is, she'll box your ears. That's why she hates me –'
'Because you don't tell her she's pretty. But she is pretty.'

The sequel to this, when Bevis returns from asking Frances to sew more sails, is also omitted.

Chatper XXV (*XX* Sampson Low)   'Sailing continued – The Pinta – New Formosa'

The choice of names for the island is shortened in the Sampson Low version. The discussion about getting a gun made is also considerably pruned.

Chapter XXVI (*XXI* Sampson Low)   'Making a Gun – The Cave'

No significant difference between the two texts.

Chapter XXVII (*XXII* Sampson Low)   'Building the Hut'

The dialogue between Mark and Bevis, after the hut is finished when they talk about living there till their beards grow down to their waists and discuss the idea of discovering gold, 'Birds of Paradise'. 'Spices and Magic things' is omitted from the Sampson Low version. The conversation during the sail is also trimmed, leaving out all talk of magic and curious things.

Chapter XXVIII (*XXIII* Sampson Low)   'Provisioning the Cave'

The dialogue when Mark and Bevis are discussing being ship-wrecked and remembering how Ulysses clung to a rock is cut to a very business-like discussion of their needs:

> 'We must bring all our things – the gun and powder, and provisions, and great-coats, and the astralobe, and spreads and leave them all here.'

There are very few changes of Jefferies's text, the editing tending to be either simple omission or condensation, however Jefferies's line referring to Frances:

> 'She shall have a bird of paradise for her hat,'

is altered in the Sampson Low version to:

> 'She shall have a bird's wing for her hat.'

Again the tendency of the Sampson Low edition is to be more matter of fact and down to earth. The dialogue between Val, little Charlie, Mark and Bevis is, slightly pruned.

Chapter XXIX (*XXIV* Sampson Low)   'More Cargoes – All Ready'

> 'If Val's watching,' said Bevis, as they came up the bank with the rugs, the last part of the load, 'he'll have to be smashed.'
> 'People who spy about ought to be killed,' said Mark.
> 'Everything ought to be done openly,' carefully depositing the concealed barrel in the stern-sheets. This was the most important thing of all. When they had got the matchlock safe in the cave, they felt that the greatest difficulty was surmounted.

This short exchange near the beginning of the chapter is omitted from the Sampson Low edition.

Chapter XXX (XXV Sampson Low) 'New Formosa'

Some of the argument between Mark and Bevis over the success of their gun and Bevis's assertion of his rank of captain is trimmed in the Sampson Low text. This is perhaps the truest piece of condensing so far. Nothing is cut from this chapter that is not restated somewhere else.

Chapter XXXI (XXVI Sampson Low) 'New Formosa – First Day'

The discussion as to the shooting powers of the gun is halved in the Sampson Low text. While the rest of the dialogue in the chapter is also considerably shortened losing such displays of imagination as the fact that New Formosa has a different time to the ordinary world:

'While it's tea-time here, it's breakfast there.'

their return home years later:

'. . . .Then some day they'll see two strange men with very long beards and bronzed faces.'

and again 'Curious magic things':

'Genii'
'Ghouls'
'Vampires. Look, there's a big bat – and another; they're coming back again'.
'That's nothing; everything's magic. Mice are magic especially if they're red. I'll show you in Faust. If they're only dun they're not half so magic.'

Chapter XXXII (XXVII Sampson Low) 'New Formosa – Morning in the Tropics'

The magic at the beginning of this chapter:

'Green eyes glaring at you in the black wood,' said Bevis.
'Huge creatures, with prickles on their backs, and stings: the ground heaves underneath, and up they come; one claw first – you see it poking through a chink – and then hot poisonous breath –'

etc., is missing from the Sampson Low version. A reference to 'the genie' when Mark wakes up is carefully removed and the conversation about how to determine the south is also missing. The references to 'Magic' and 'Enchantment' at the end of the chapter are included in both texts.

Chapter XXXIII (*XXVIII* Sampson Low)   'New Formosa – Planning the Raft'

The dialogue at the beginning of the chapter where Mark and Bevis discuss future exploration is reduced to a much more matter of fact statement in the Sampson Low version.

> He thought of the huge boa-constrictors hidden in the interior of New Formosa – they would be basking quite still in such heat, but he ought to have brought his spear with him. You never ought to venture from the stockade in these unknown places without a spear. By now the shadows had moved, and his foot was in the sunshine: he could feel the heat through the leather. Two bubbles came up to the surface close to the shore: he saw the second one start from the sand and rise up quickly with a slight wobble, but the sand did not move, and he could not see anything in it.

The above paragraph is removed from near the end of the chapter for the Sampson Low version.

Chapter XXXIV (*XXIX* Sampson Low)   'New Formosa – Kangaroos'

The descriptive passages in this chapter are virtually the same in both texts but the dialogue is considerably shortened in the Sampson Low version.

Chapter XXXV (*XXX* Sampson Low)   'New Formosa – Bevis's Zodiac'

The whole of the imaginative conversation while Bevis is writing up the journal is omitted from the Sampson Low edition, as is the bulk of this chapter dealing with Bevis's Zodiac, the Sampson Low edition includes under this title the events described in the next chapter.

Chapter XXVI   'New Formosa – The Raft'

The dialogue when they are heaving the boat down to the water is slightly shortened. The references to possible crocodiles are removed from the closing paragraphs.

Chapter XXXVII (*XXXI* Sampson Low)   'New Formosa – No Hope of Returning'

The dialogue of this chapter is heavily cut in the Sampson Low text.

Chapter XXXVIII (*XXXII* Sampson Low)   'New Formosa – Something has been to the Hut'

The more fanciful suggestions as to what has stolen their food, such as 'Lions', 'Tigers', 'Boas' and 'Panthers' are omitted from the Sampson Low version, while the English birds and animals 'Foxes', 'Eagles' and 'Cats' are retained. Again suggestions of 'magic' are removed. The dialogue at the end of the chapter where Mark asks Bevis to tell him a story and the story which is the next chapter are omitted from the Sampson Low version.

Chapter XXXIX   'New Formosa – The Story of the Other Side'

Bevis relates the story of a traveller who visits Tibet, and is shown a bronze door which leads into a magical country to which there is no other side. The only portion of this chapter which is retained in the Sampson Low version is the final paragraph:

> Watching the swan among the glittering ripples, they cracked the rest of the nuts, and did not get up to go till the sun was getting low. It was not a wild swan, but one whose feathers had not been clipped. The wind rose a little, and sighed dreamily through the tops of the tall firs as they walked under them. They returned along the shore, where the weeds came to the island, and had gone some way, when Mark suddenly caught hold of Bevis and drew him behind a bush.

Chapter XL (XXXIII Sampson Low) 'New Formosa – The Matchlock'

Again the dialogue is heavily cut and as this reveals much of the make-believe world of the boys the result is a more straightforward but less poetic narrative combining this chapter with the next.

Chapter XLI   'New Formosa – Sweet River Falls'

Chapter XLII (XXXIV Sampson Low) 'New Formosa – The Mainland'

Again the dialogue is almost entirely removed and the boys' make-believe world reduced, e.g.:

> 'We might have been tortured,' said Mark, as they stepped on the raft. 'Tied up and gimlets bored into our heads'.
> 'The king of this country is an awful tyrant,' said Bevis.
> 'Very likely he would have fixed us in a hollow tree and smeared us with honey and let the flies eat us.'
> 'Unless we could save his daughter, who is ill, and all the magicians can't do her any good.'
> 'Now they are hoping we shall come with a wonderful talisman. We must study magic – we keep on putting if off; I wonder if there really is a jewel in the toad's head.'

'You have not inked the wizard's foot on the gateway', said Mark.

Chapter XLIII (*XXXV* Sampson Low) 'New Formosa –The Something comes again'

The dialogue is very slightly shortened and the following poetic paragraph is omitted from the Sampson Low version:

> In the butchery of the Wars of the Roses, that such flowers should be stained with such memories! It is certain that the murderers watched the robin perched hard by. He listened to the voice of fair Rosamond; he was at the tryst where Amy Robsart met her lover. Nothing happens in the fields and woods without a robin.

Chapter XLIV (*XXXVI* Sampson Low) 'New Formosa – The Tiger from the Reeds'

Again the dialogue of the Sampson Low edition is considerably shortened, but the narrative passages are virtually the same in both texts.

Chapter XLV (*XXXVII* Sampson Low) 'New Formosa – The Fortification'

Two pages of dialogue about the tiger hunt is reduced in the Sampson Low edition to:

> The boy's spirits rose, and he felt ready for anything.

At this point the method of editing seems to have stabilised, as has been noted above the cutting seems now to be confined almost entirely to the dialogue. This is not the pattern of the earlier chapters. The evidence seems to point towards a lack of revision of the cutting.

Chapter XLVI (*XXXVIII* Sampson Low) 'New Formosa – The Trail'

This chapter is virtually identical in both texts. However the Sampson Low version runs straight on into the next chapter without any division.

Chapter XLVII 'New Formosa – Voyage in the Calypso'

The pattern of cutting the dialogue by approximately half is repeated in this chapter.

Chapter XLVIII (*XXXIX* Sampson Low) 'New Formosa – The Captive'

As well as the usual trimming of the dialogue certain meditative paragraphs not essential to the narrative but essential to Jefferies' intention are removed, e.g.

> I do not know how any can slumber with this over them; how any can look down at the clods. The greatest wonder on earth is that there are any not able to see the earth's surpassing beauty. Such moments are beyond the chronograph and any measure of wheels; the passing of one cog may be equal to a century, for the mind has no time. What an incredible marvel it is that there are human creatures that slumber three score and ten years, and look down at the clods and then say, 'We are old, we have lived seventy years.' Seventy years! The passing of one cog is longer; seven hundred times seventy years would not equal the click of the tiniest cog while the mind was living its own life. Sleep and clods, with the glory of the earth, and the sun, and the sea, and the endless ether around us! Incredible marvel this sleep and clods and talk of years. But I suppose it was only a second or two, for some slight movement attracted him, and he looked, and instantly the vision above was forgotten.

Chapter XLIX (*XL* Sampson Low)   'New Formosa – The Black Sail'

The section near the beginning of the chapter which discusses some of the things said by Bevis as a little boy, which his mother had noted on the fly-leaves of her prayer book is omitted. We lose such gems as:

> 'If God had a pussy?'

and after he was told that God loved little boys:

> 'But does He love ladies too?'

or when seeing the Houses of Parliament for the first time and being reminded of his toy bricks, he inquired:

> 'If there was anything inside?'

Again material of this kind is not essential to the story, it even slows the narrative but Jefferies intention was to create a mood and show a true picture of childhood rather than simply tell a story. The Sampson Low edition cuts from the first two paragraphs of Chapter L to Chapter LII which it includes almost unchanged; all this is included in this chapter without further division.

Chapter L   'Shooting with Double-Barrels'

Chapter LI   'American Snap-shooting'

Chapter LII   'The Antarctic Expedition — Conclusion'

Appendix   'The Ballad of King Estmere'; 'The Secret of the Sea' by Longfellow.

There is nothing here that conflicts with Henty's known style. The main features are a good sense of narrative, a desire to 'get on with the story', and a feeling that this abridgement was done virtually at a sitting. Henty never rewrote his stories dictating them to an amanuensis and not checking them again till he saw them in proof. Chapter IX contains the most typical Henty touch but as the text is cut rather than rewritten there are not sufficient paragraphs by the editor to compare these with Henty's known style, even so it is cut as one would expect from Henty and massive alteration of the original text would be out of character for Henty. I think we can safely presume that this one volume edition is edited by Henty and that there is in fact no edition bearing his name.

A final connection between Jefferies and Henty is that they both contributed to *The Standard*. The preface to *Hodge and His Masters* by R. Jefferies, London, Smith, Elder and Co. 1880 (2 vols):

> The papers of which these volumes are composed originally appeared in *The Standard*, and are now republished by permission of the Editor.

Chapter ii

The Battle of Tel-el-Kebir

Henty is known to have been employed by the *Standard*, after his days as an active war correspondent were over, to rewrite telegrams received from other correspondents. A comparison between the description of the battle of Tel-el-Kebir prepared by him for the 1883 edition of *Our Soldiers* and the description of the same battle 'from the *Standard*, Sept. 14, 1882' as rendered in *The Standard Author English History* George Gill & Sons (*c.* 1882) would seem to bear this out.

Standard Author History

The most complete success has attended our attack upon the enemy's position, and not only has Tel-el-Kebir fallen into our hands but the Egyptian army has ceased to exist. When I despatched my telegram yesterday evening, the troops were all at work striking and rolling up tents, packing baggage, and carrying everything to the side of the railway. That duty finished, they fell in.

The first move was a short one, being only to the sandhills above the camp. There arms were piled, and the men lay down on the sand, or sat and

Our Soldiers

On the 12th the whole expeditionary force was assembled at Kassassin, and in the evening the camp was struck, and the army, 14,000 strong, moved out and, piling their arms, lay down on the sand until one o'clock; then they again fell into rank and advanced.

Scarcely a word was spoken, and the dark columns moved off almost noiselessly, their footfalls being deadened by the sand.

chatted quietly over the coming fight. At one o'clock the word was passed round, and they again fell in. Never did a body of fourteen thousand men get under arms more quietly; the very orders appeared to be given in lowered tones, and almost noiselessly the dark columns moved off, their footfalls being deadened by the sand. The silence, broken only by the occasional clash of steel, the certainty that the great struggle would commence with the dawn, and the expectation that at any moment we might be challenged by the Bedouin horsemen, far out in the plain in front of the enemy, all combined to make it an impressive march, and one which none who shared it will ever forget.

There were frequent halts to enable the regiments to maintain touch, and to allow the transport waggons, whose wheels crunched over the sandy plains, with a noise which to our ears seemed strangely loud, to keep up with us. On our right was Graham's brigade, which has already done good service by twice repelling the assaults of the enemy upon this camp. Next to them came the Guards' brigade, which was, when the action began, to act in support of that of Graham. Between these and the Canal moved the forty-two guns of the Royal Artillery under General Goodenough. On the railway

On the right was Graham's Brigade, which had already done such good service by twice repelling the assaults of the enemy: Next to them came the brigade of Guards, which was, when the action began, to act as their support; Next to these moved 42 guns of the Royal Artillery, and on the line of railway the Naval Brigade advance with the 40-pounder on a truck; beside them came the Highland Brigade, –

Standard Author History   *Our Soldiers*

itself the naval brigade advanced with a forty-pounder on a truck. South of the Canal the Highland brigades led the advance, followed by the Indian troops in support. The cavalry and horse artillery had started due north, to make a long detour, and to come down upon the enemy's line of retreat.

By early dawn the troops had arrived within a thousand yards of the enemy's line, and halted there for a short time to enable the fighting line to be formed, and other preparations to be made. A perfect silence still reigned over the plain, and it was difficult to credit the fact that some fourteen thousand men lay in a semi-circle round the enemy's lines, ready to dash forward at a signal to the low sandy heaps in front, behind which twice as many men slumbered, unsuspicious of the presence of their foes. As is usual in a movement carried out in the darkness, many detached parties altogether lost their way. I was with the mounted police, and for a while we completely lost the rest of the force, and moved hither and thither all night, until just at daybreak we nearly stumbled in to the enemy's lines.

The attack began on our left, and nothing could be imagined finer than the advance of the Highland brigade. The 74th were next to the Canal; next to them were the Cameronians;

– the Cameronians, 74th Gordon Highlanders, and the Black Watch, – the 46th and 60th forming their support. It was upon these that the brunt of the action fell. So silent was the advance in the darkness, that the enemy did not perceive the advancing column until they were within 300 yards. The Highlanders were advancing to attack the face of the works nearest to the line of march and consequently arrived at their destination some time before Graham's Brigade, which had to make a sweep round. Suddenly a terrific fire broke from the Egyptian entrenchment upon the Highlanders. Not a shot was fired in reply, but with a wild cheer the Highland regiment dashed at the enemy's line.

Against so fierce and rapid an onslaught the Egyptians could make but little stand, and the Highlanders dashed over the line of earthworks. Scarcely, however, had they won that

Standard Author History   *Our Soldiers*

the Gordon Highlanders continued the line, with the Black Watch upon their flank. The 46th and 60th formed the second line.

Swiftly and silently the Highlanders moved forward to the attack. No word was spoken, no shot fired, until within three hundred yards of the enemy's earthworks, nor up to that time did a sound in the Egyptian lines betoken that they were aware of the presence of their assailants. Then suddenly a terrific fire flashed along the line of sand heaps and a storm of bullets whizzed over the heads of the advancing troops. A wild cheer broke from the Highlanders in response, the pipes struck shrilly up, bayonets were fixed, and at the double this splendid body of men dashed forward.

The first line of entrenchments was carried, the enemy offering scarce any resistance, but from another line of entrenchments behind, which in the still dim light could be scarcely seen, a burst of musketry broke out. For a few minutes the Highlanders poured in a heavy fire in

position when the Egyptians opened a tremendous fire from an entrenchment further back. The Highlanders for a minute or two replied, and then advanced again at a charge. The Egyptians fought stoutly, and for a time a hand-to-hand struggle went on; then some of the Highlanders penetrated by an opening between the Egyptian entrenchments, and opened fire upon their flank.

This was too much for them, and they almost immediately broke and fled.

In the meantime fighting had begun on the other flank, warned by the roar of conflict with the Highlanders. The Egyptians were here prepared, and for a time kept up a steady fire upon our troops. The 18th Royal Irish were sent to turn the enemy's left, and dashed at the trenches, exchange; but it was probably as innocuous as that of the unseen enemy, whose bullets whistled harmlessly overhead. The delay of the advance was but a short one. Soon the order was given, and the brigade again went rapidly forward.

Soon a portion of the force had passed between the enemy's redoubts, and opened a flanking fire upon him. This was too much for the Egyptians, who at once took to their heels, and fairly ran, suffering, as the crowded masses rushed across the open, very heavily from our fire, being literally mown down by hundreds.

Meanwhile the fighting had begun upon the other flank. The horse artillery shelled the enemy's extreme left. Here the Egyptians seemed more prepared than they had been on their right, and for a time kept up a steady fire. The 18th Royal Irish were sent between the enemy's left, under the guidance of Major Hart, who accompanied them as staff officer and at the word dashed at the trenches, and carried them at the bayonet's point, so turning the flank of defenders of the position. Next to the 18th came the 87th, and next to them the 84th, the Guards being close behind in support. These regiments advanced by regular rushes. For a short time the enemy clung to his line of entrenchments, but his fire was

carrying them at the bayonet's point. Next to the 18th came the 87th and 84th, with the Guards close behind.

For a short time the enemy clung to the line of entrenchments, but their fire was very ineffective.

Standard Author History   *Our Soldiers*

singularly ineffective, and our troops got fairly into the trenches in front of them. Then the enemy fought stoutly for a few moments, and the combat was hand to hand. Major Hart shot one man as he was trying to wrest his revolver from his hand, and this, even after the trench had been turned by our advance on their flank. Then, as our troops poured in, the Egyptians fled as rapidly as those on the other side of the Canal had done before the Highlanders.

The fight was now practically over, the only further danger arising from bullets our own troops who were firing in all directions upon the fleeing enemy, as with loud cheers our whole line advanced in pursuit. The Egyptians did not preserve the slightest semblance of order, but fled in a confused rabble at the top of their speed. As we descended the hill leading down to Tel-el-Kebir station, we captured the standing camp, with immense stores of forage and provisions.

By this time the Highland division was already in their camp, and soon losing heart they too fled, and the whole Egyptian army were in full rout.

It should be noted that the above comparison does not establish Henty's editorial or sub-editorial involvement in the *Standard* account. He repeatedly acknowledges the fact that he drew on eye-witness accounts of campaigns in which he was not involved. It does, however, establish a strong enough connection to justify the inclusion of both accounts in any Henty collections and future bibliographies should include a note to this effect at the end of the entry for *Our Soldiers*.

Chapter iii

Henty's Illustrators

W. BOUCHER

Courage and Conflict 1901
Gallant Deeds 1905 (from *Brains* and *Bravery* and *Courage and Conflict*)
Peril and Prowess 1899
Venture and Valour 1900

Died March 5 1906; associate of the Royal Society of Painters, Etchers and Engravers. Exhibited in the Royal Academy from 1888 to 1891.

MAYNARD BROWN

By Pike and Dyke 1890(1889)

Painter mainly of historical scenes, he lived in Nottingham. He exhibited at the Royal Academy and other London galleries from 1878 onwards.

GORDON BROWNE

Bonnie Prince Charlie 1888 (1887)
By Sheer Pluck 1884 (1883)
Facing Death 1882 (1881)
For Name and Fame 1886 (1885)
Held Fast for England 1892 (1891)
In Freedom's Cause 1885 (1884)
The Lion of St Mark 1889 (1888)
Orange and Green 1888 (1887)
St George for England 1885 (1884)
True to the Old Flag 1885 (1884)
Under Drake's Flag 1883 (1882)

With Clive in India 1884 (1883)
With Lee in Virginia 1890 (1889)
With Wolfe in Canada 1887 (1886)

Born on April 15 1858, he was the son of 'Phiz' the illustrator of several of Dicken's works. His first book illustration was in 1875 (A. R. Hope's *The Day After the Holidays*). His tutor, James Cooper, introduced him to Blackie's for whom he illustrated an incredible amount, including the above titles by Henty. He was also associated with the *Boys Own Paper*, (illustrating among other titles, T. B. Reed's *The Adventures of a Three Guinea Watch*,) *Chums* and *The Captain*. He drew for many adult magazines and was one of the most prolific of Victorian book illustrators. He exhibited at the Royal Academy and the Royal Institute. He was a member of the Royal Society of British Artists and also of the Royal Institute of painters in Water-Colours. He died in 1932.

HERBERT JAMES DRAPER

St Bartholomew's Eve 1894 (1893)

Landscape and figure painter born 1864. He first exhibited at the Royal Academy in 1887. He also exhibited at the Paris *Exposition Universelle* in 1900. There are paintings by him in the National Gallery and the Liverpool Museum.

FRANCES EVAN

A Soldier's Daughter 1906 (1905)

No details available.

JOSEPH FINNEMORE

When London Burned 1895 (1894)

Born in Birmingham in 1860. He travelled extensively in Russia to study painting. He regularly exhibited portraits and paintings at the Royal Academy.

ROBERT FOWLER

Sturdy and Strong 1888 (1887)

Born in Anstruther in Fife in 1853. He became associated with Liverpool, three paintings being preserved in the Liverpool Museum. Other examples are in the museums of Bootle and Magdebourg. He was an Associate of the Royal Cambrian Academy and a Member of the Royal Institute of Painters in Water Colour. He frequently exhibited in London, from 1876, particularly at the Royal Academy and the Royal Institute.

HARRY FURNISS

Seaside Maidens 1880

Born in Ireland in 1854. He was a member of the staff of *Punch*. His early work includes drawings for Thackeray's *Ballads* and *The Rose and the Ring* alongside work by Thackeray and Du Maurier. He illustrated Lewis Carroll's *Sylvie and Bruno* and *Sylvie and Bruno concluded*. A member of the Savage Club, he was a great social personality. He died in 1925.

WILLIAM H. C. GROOME

Dash and Daring 1898
Hazard and Heroism 1904
Steady and Strong 1905

A member of the Royal Society of British Artists. His paintings were regularly exhibited after 1881.

PAUL HARDY

A Jacobite Exile 1894 (1893)

Active as early as 1864 when he illustrated Macaulay's *Lays of Ancient Rome* for Nister.

GODFREY C. HINDLEY

In the Heart of the Rockies 1895 (1894)

Well known as a painter of flowers. A member of the Royal Institute of Oil Painters. One of his paintings is in the Sunderland Museum. He exhibited at the Royal Academy from 1876.

HAL HURST

Through the Sikh War 1894 (1893)
A Woman of the Commune first illustrated edition 1896

Born 1865, he was a well known painter, water-colour painter and miniature painter, being a member of the Society of British Artists, the Royal Institute of Painters in Water-Colours and the Royal Society of Miniature Painters. He took part in the 1900 Paris *Exposition Universelle*.

J. JELLICOE

In the Hands of the Malays 1905 (1904)

No details available about this artist.

ROBERT THOMAS LANDELLS

The Young Franc-Tireurs 1872

Landells was one of the artists on the staff of the *Illustrated London News*. Son of the wood-engraver, Ebenezer Landells, who

was one of the founder members of the staff of *Punch* and also
employed by the *Illustrated London News*. R. T. was born in 1833
and died in 1877. Almost certainly a personal friend of Henty he
covered several campaigns for the *Illustrated London News* including the Crimean and Franco-Prussian Wars.

WILLIAM HENRY MARGETSON

A March on London 1897 (1896)
With Cochrane the Dauntless 1897 (1896)

A member of the Society of Oil Painters. He exhibited at the
Royal Academy. There is a painting of his in Sydney Musuem.

WAT MILLER

In the Hands of the Cave-Dwellers 1903 (1902)

No details of this artist available.

JOSEPH NASH, R.I.

The Dash for Khartoum 1892 (1891)

A celebrated artist of this name exhibited in London from 1831.
His paintings are to be found in many museums, particularly the
Victoria and Albert and the British Museum.

Possibly Joseph Nash, R.I., is his son although there is a
nineteenth-century illustrator John Nash who is sometimes confused with his more famous namesake.

WILLIAM HEYSMAN OVEREND

A Chapter of Adventures 1891 (1890)
One of the 28th 1890 (1889)
On the Irrawaddy 1897 (1896)
Through Russian Snows 1896 (1895)

Born 1851, died 1898. One of the best known illustrators for the
Illustrated London News. He was a member of the Royal Institute
of Painters in Oil Colours and exhibited at the Royal Academy
from 1872.

HENRY MARRIETT PAGET

Bravest of the Brave 1887 (1886)
Captain Bayley's Heir 1889 (1888)
Through the Fray 1886 (1885)

Born 1857, died 1936. Brother of Wal and Sidney, who created
the features of Sherlock Holmes. Collaborated with others in
Nister's *Pictures from Dickens* 1895.

WAL PAGET

At Agincourt 1897 (1896)
At the Point of the Bayonet 1902 (1901)
Condemned as a Nihilist 1893 (1892)
Through three Campaigns 1904 (1903)
The Treasure of the Incas 1903 (1902)
Under Wellington's Command 1899 (1898)
With Frederick the Great 1898 (1897)
With Moore at Corunna 1898 (1897)
With the Allies to Pekin 1904 (1903)
With the British Legion 1903 (1902)

Born 1863, died 1935. As well as his work for Blackie he illustrated Scott and Stevenson for Ward Lock and Cassell. One of the most prolific of late Victorian illustrators he took over from Gordon Browne as Henty's main illustrator.

W. PARKINSON

Beric the Briton 1892 (1891)

No information available about this artist.

RALPH PEACOCK

Both Sides the Border 1899 (1898)
A Knight of the White Cross 1896 (1895)
Wulf the Saxon 1895 (1894)

Won a bronze medal at the 1900, Paris, *Exposition Universelle*. His *portrait of William Holman Hunt* is in the Liverpool Museum. Exhibited regularly at the Royal Academy and at Suffolk Street from 1888.

ALFRED PEARSE

By England's Aid 1891 (1890)
Maori and Settler 1891 (1890)
Redskin and Cowboy 1892 (1891)

No details of this artist available.

HORACE WILLIAM PETHERICK

The Cornet of Horse 1881

Born 1839, died 1919. Exhibited in London between 1877 and 1901.

ERNEST PRATER

The Lost Heir 1899

No details available for this artist.

JOHN PROCTOR

The Young Buglers 1880
Yarns on the Beach 1886 (1885)

No details available tor this artist.

ARTHUR RACKHAM A.R.W.S.

Brains and Bravery 1903
Gallant Deeds 1905 (from *Brains and Bravery* and *Courage and Conflict*)

Born in 1867 he is one of the most celebrated of illustrators. Usually his drawings have an eerie unworldly quality, with trees, witches, goblins and gnarled figures, the two titles above are quite different from his usual style, being typical Henty illustrations. This is the more remarkable as he had already come into prominence with his illustrations for the *Ingoldsby Legends* (1898), *Grimms Fairy Tales* (1900) and *Gulliver's Travels* (1900). He died in 1939 while still working on a new edition of *The Wind in the Willows*.

WILLIAM RAINEY, R.I.

At Aboukir and Acre 1899 (1898)
By Conduct and Courage 1905 (1904)
Grit and Go 1902
Out with Garibaldi 1901 (1900)
A Roving Commission 1900 (1899)
With Buller in Natal 1900 (1901)
With Kitchener in the Soudan 1903 (1902)
With Roberts to Pretoria 1902 (1901)

Born 1852, died 1936. A member of the Royal Institute of Painters in Water-Colours from 1891. He won a bronze medal at the 1900 Paris *Exposition Universelle*. He exhibited at the Royal Academy and the Suffolk Street Gallery from 1876. He also wrote at least four adventure stories for boys.

J. SCHÖNBERG

In the Reign of Terror 1888 (1887)
The Lion of the North 1886 (1885)

Possibly Johann Nepomuk Schönberg, an Austrian painter and illustrator born in 1844, but no certain details available.

CHARLES M. SHELDON

In the Irish Brigade 1901 (1900)
To Herat and Cabul 1902 (1901)
Won by the Sword 1900 (1899)

No details of this artist available.

JOSEPH J. SOLOMON or SOLOMON J. SOLOMON, R.I., R.A.

For the Temple 1888 (1887)

Born 1854, died 1927. Studied in Paris and London. Travelled in Italy, Germany, Holland, Spain and Morocco. Exhibited in London from 1881.

LANCELOT SPEED

frontispiece *In Battle and Breeze* 1896

Born 1860, died 1932. Collaborated with H. J. Ford in Andrew Lang's series of *Fairy Books*.

PERCY F. S. SPENCE

A Hidden Foe (1 vol edition) 1901

Born in Sydney 1868, died in London 1933. Passed the early part of his life in Fiji and first exhibited in the exhibitions of the Art Society of New South Wales. He worked for the *Graphic* and *Punch*. His painting of Robert Louis Stevenson is in the National Gallery.

W. S. STACEY

By Right of Conquest 1891 (1890)
In Greek Waters 1893 (1892)

Born 1846, died 1929. He exhibited in London from 1871 at the Royal Academy and Suffolk Street. He was a member of the Royal Institute of Painters in Water-Colours.

CHARLES JOSEPH STANILAND, R.I.

The Dragon and the Raven 1886 (1885)
The Young Carthaginian 1887 (1886)

Born at Kingston-upon-Hull in 1838. He studied at Birmingham and London. The Victoria and Albert Museum and the Sunderland Art Gallery possess water-colours by him.

SIMON H. VEDEER

The Young Colonists 1897 (1896) Blackie Edition

No details of this artist available.

JOHN REINHARD WEGUELIN

The Cat of Bubastes

Born 1849, died 1927. He exhibited in London, notably at the Royal Academy from 1877. He also illustrated *Hans Anderson's Fairy Tales* for Lawrence and Bullen and an edition of the *Lays of Ancient Rome* for Longmans in 1881. There is a painting of his in the Cape Town Museum.

HARRISON WILLIAM WEIR

Those Other Animals (1891)

Born 1824, died 1906. A pupil of George Baxter, he concentrated on pictures of birds and animals. He wrote and illustrated *Poultry and All About Them*. He contributed to the *Illustrated London News* and the *Graphic*. He exhibited in London between 1843 and 1880, notably at the Royal Academy.

WILLIAM BARNES WOLLEN

A Final Reckoning 1887 (1886)

A member of the Royal Institute. He exhibited in London from 1879, notably at the Royal Institute and the Royal Academy. He obtained a silver medal at the 1889 Paris exhibition.

STANLEY L. WOOD

No Surrender! 1900 (1899)
Rujub the Juggler one volume edition 1893

One of the most prolific of late Victorian illustrators, illustrating books by Henty's successors, Captain Brereton and others, particularly for Blackie.

JOHANN-BAPTIST ZWECKER or ZWEECKER

Out on the Pampas 1871 (1870)

Born in Frankfurt in 1814, died in London in 1876. He studied at the Institute Stadel. He continued his studies in Dusseldorf. He settled in London where he illustrated on *Alphabet of Animals* 1861, *An Alphabet of Birds* 1861, and several fairy stories and books for young people.

Huson, 32*
Boys Brigade, 24